From
GOOD MAN
to
VALIANT MAN

SEXUAL INTEGRITY IN A SEX CRAZY WORLD

DR ALLAN MEYER

To Chris,
Proud to serve alongside
in NSW.
Be blessed Myer

PRAISE FOR VALIANT MAN

This book is a further development of the material presented in Valiant Man – a 10 week teaching and small group experience for men. Why write a program like Valiant Man? Because I am a survivor and I'm grateful.

At the year of first publishing this book (2008) the Valiant Man program is a little over three years old. It has been embraced all over Australia and has made its way into New Zealand, North America, South Africa and many other places around the world. I have met thousands of the men who have participated in the Valiant Man program and their stories have moved me to tears. Men struggle to manage their relentless sex drive well. When they fail the price tag can be catastrophic. When they succeed the world is a better place.

I have succeeded and I am grateful. This year my wife Helen and I celebrate our 40th wedding anniversary. I love my wife and she loves me back. However, I have not succeeded without a struggle. I wrote this book because men need help. Both the Valiant Man course and this book, *From Good Man to Valiant Man*, can be the beginning of a new life – a life in which marriages prosper, women and children dwell safely, and men walk with their heads held high.

I am proud of the men who have taken the development of their sexual integrity seriously. Here are some of their stories:

"Thank you for Valiant Man; it saved my life, marriage and soul." [Arizona, USA]

"I am a college student at Hillsong College Sydney. I took part in Valiant Man and, to cut a long story short, became free from 8 years of pornography addiction and distortions. Following this I am living in such an incredible new place of life, which is surely God's healing and grace. I will never be the same and this is a defining part of my faith, I am so thankful to your ministry and to God for His revelation to you." [Sydney, Australia.]

"Thank you so much for opening our eyes. I want to tell you that the biggest thing I got out of this…is HOPE. As a group, we have talked about our struggles and we know that we struggle, but we didn't exactly understand why and what to do about it." [California, USA]

"I am 83. If this course had been available 70 years ago and I understood how valuable it was I would have paid $100,000 for it no kidding. Imagine the pain and damage that would have been averted. My life would have been totally different." [New Zealand]

"I am writing to you particularly now about your teaching entitled Valiant Man. Let me start by thanking you from the bottom of my heart for writing it. I praise God that he really did an awesome work through you and the ministry of that teaching.

From a very young age I found myself addicted to all types of porn from mainstream, to fetish, to lesbian, and just some downright abominable pornographic media. I found myself using drugs in my teens and up until only four months ago practiced compulsive, serial masturbation up to four times a day. I was a seriously depraved individual, allowing my every whim to be entertained, spiraling down and down until my sexuality and views of sexual practices resembled that of the era and practices of Sodom and Gomorrah.

I wanted to share my sexual testimony with you to illustrate that a person can be truly changed and touched by your teaching in a way that even you thought might not be possible. I can say that through your teaching, God has given me much strength and understanding. I no longer masturbate at all and haven't since a few nights before I started the program here. I particularly found the journaling helpful. I found that the DVD teaching and notes were effectively coupled with the 'hands on' approach of journaling and the small group accountability we shared.

I would like to finish by saying that your teaching offered me hope. It offered me hope that there is a way out of my sexual deviancy and perversion, and that with a little perseverance, a lot of patience and the employing of all relevant Valiant Man strategies I can truly become a Valiant Man and even sexually disciple others in similar circumstances. Thank you Allan, from a changed student." [Teen Challenge, Victoria, Australia.]

"I was mistreating my girlfriend and had terrible attitudes to women. The Valiant Man course totally changed my view of manhood and sexuality. I now treat my girlfriend with the dignity she deserves and we are engaged to be married". [Christchurch, New Zealand]

I could have filled the book with stories, but the most important one is yet to be written – yours!

So let's enter the fray together.
See you at the other end of the book.

Allan R Meyer

CONTENTS

INTRODUCTION

A VISION FOR MANHOOD

"What is life but the angle of vision? A man is measured by
the angle at which he looks at objects. What is life but what a
man is thinking of all day? This is his fate and his employer.
Knowing is the measure of the man. By how much we know, so
much we are."
Ralph Waldo Emerson

"What happens to a man is less significant than what
happens within him."
Louis L. Mann

What is *the 21st century man?* What is manhood meant to look like today? A few decades ago a tobacco company successfully promoted the Marlboro Man as the ideal man. He was rugged, unshaven, and he squinted through a haze of cigarette smoke. More recently Western civilization has portrayed the ideal man as a SNAG—a Sensitive New Age Guy, a man who knows how to dress, smell, hug and speak without offending anybody.

For you it may be Tiger Woods or Brad Pitt or even the Dalai Lama. The truth is that in western society today men are being bombarded from almost every direction with visions of what it means to be a man in the 21st century. Whether we like it or not, our role models tend to be sports stars, movie celebrities, CEOs of multinational corporations, political leaders and even religious leaders.

But *what* and *who* is to be our example of true manhood today? Every man needs a clear picture of what true manhood looks like. Every man needs a vision of what he is intended to be. The Book of Proverbs tells us, "Where there is no prophetic vision the people cast off restraint..."[1] Across many nations today men are doing exactly that. Men are living unrestrained lives because they are not really sure of what it is they are supposed to be. When a man doesn't know what he is meant to be, it gives him a lot of options as to how he can choose to live. He never feels like he is missing the mark because he never knows where he is meant to be headed anyway.

And yet, deep within each man's heart, there is a moral core that continually weighs choices and motives in the balance and judges how life is being lived. When a man suspects that he's not all that he could be or should be, it has a huge impact on the way he handles responsibility, the way he relates to God, the way he treats women, and the way he feels about himself.

---

1   Proverbs 29:18, ESV

This book is about personal purity. It's about managing libido and sexual passions well, and for every man that's a challenge. If I've learned anything in life it's the fact that even good men find their sexual passions a struggle. I've seen too many good men yield to the pressure and subsequently damage themselves and the people for whom they were responsible. It happened all too often to good men who are part of the Bible story. Look at King David; he was a very good man who caved in to sexual pressure and destroyed the lives of people who were counting on him as their leader. Like David, there may be men, women and children who are counting on you for guidance, for friendship, for spiritual and emotional support, for leadership, and for strength of character. They need you to be better than good. They need you to go beyond being a *good* man to become a *valiant* man.

That's my challenge to you: Would you be willing to progress from *good* man to *valiant* man? It takes a *valiant* man to pursue with courage the vision of manhood that God has set before each one of us. It takes a *valiant* man to face the deep painful change necessary to deal with distortions that have crept in and taken a grip on his sex drive. It takes a *valiant* man to be a consistent, long-term blessing to those who rely on him, whether that's his family, his close friends, his work colleagues, his employees, or those who follow his spiritual leadership.

The difference between a *good* man and a *valiant* man

There is a big difference between being a *good* man and a *valiant* man. King Solomon was a good man; he was called to be King of Israel at its greatest point in history. As a young man, God invited Solomon to ask Him for anything he wanted. What would you have asked for? Well, Solomon asked God for wisdom. He knew that as the young leader of Israel he lacked the experience and capacity necessary to manage that responsibility well; so he cried out for wisdom. Only a good man would make a choice like that. It was a brilliant request, and it was granted... along with a lot of other goodies. Solomon was possibly the wisest man the world had ever known—until Jesus came along. He was certainly smart enough to get a few of his books published in the Bible!

Solomon was a good man. He was a king, yet he still faced all the same pressures other men face, and he found those pressures disturbing. He watched his birthdays mount up year after year until it was painfully clear that, just like everybody before him, he was going to get old and die. As the days of his life disappeared into the sunset, 'like sands through the hour glass', he felt a growing desperation about the meaning of life. He ended up writing a book about his mounting unhappiness; it's called Ecclesiastes, which when translated from Hebrew into English means "the preacher". Even though he was King his own mortality and the routine of life bugged him. His wisdom made him a deep thinker – a philosopher if you like – and contemplating his own unhappiness allowed him to put his finger on some of the troubling challenges of manhood. Men were created for adventure and excitement, yet there is so much repetition and ordinariness in life—same job, same house, same wife, same kids, same bills, day after day after day. Even good men long for more than routine.

Yet the reality of Solomon's life was anything but routine; he was a king with the opportunity and the money to do anything his heart desired. If boredom bothered this man, it has every chance of bothering you too. In fact, the sense of ordinariness and futility that can so easily creep into a man's existence troubled him to such an extent that he decided to turn his life into a research project so that other men would know how to solve the problem of boredom and live an exciting life. Ecclesiastes chapter two is the record of this good man's research project.

How did his project unfold? Well, he tried every escape route available to a man, both then and now. He chased every distraction life had to offer: pleasure, sport, gambling, booze, business, home improvements, music and entertainment of every kind, making money, spending money on the newest and the latest things money can buy… and the most exciting past time of all—sex. This man had a harem that Hugh Hefner couldn't match.

So how did it work out for Solomon? What did living every man's dream do for him? Most men would sigh and say, "What a life!" Well, actually, it wasn't! At the conclusion of his project he stated very simply, "I hated life." I've watched a lot of good men struggle in exactly the same way, with the same disastrous results. In fact, when good men begin a search for the meaning of life outside of God's plans, they end up frustrated and hating life. Even worse, the women and children relying on them start to hate their lives as well.

That's why my dad is my hero. My dad was more than a good man, he was a *valiant man*. My dad must have felt all the same pressures Solomon felt. I say he *must* have felt them because I've felt them and I've got half his DNA! But my dad didn't react the way Solomon did. Instead of trying every escape route in life he embraced the challenges of life and the struggles of his own passions with dignity and steady reliability. My dad lived straight and true; he was a constant blessing to my mother, to his kids, to his church, and to his community. Every day my dad worked faithfully, paying his bills, treating my mother like the Queen, and making Jesus the meaning of his life. I never came home to see my mother in tears because Dad had been conducting Solomon's research project down at the local pub, trying to drown his sorrows. I never saw Mum in tears because Dad had been bored with life and had plundered the bank account to buy some new toy for himself, and now the bills couldn't be paid. A *valiant man* faces all the same issues a good man faces, but he never forgets that God, his family, his wife, his church, and his community need him to handle his struggles with honor and dignity. A *valiant man* has a prophetic vision of his manhood, and he lives it out courageously.

Would you be willing to rise above being just a *good* man to become a *valiant man*? Would you be willing to learn to stand tall, learn to face the same challenges other men face, but with the integrity and stability that takes you beyond the life of a *good* man to the life of a *valiant man*? God is looking for *valiant men* across the earth. Their numbers are yet small, but it doesn't have to stay that way. You could swell the number of valiant men in this generation if you have the willingness to do the journey.

Would it help you to have a prophetic vision of what God designed and created you to be… as a man? God has a very clear vision for what a man could be and I want to help you grasp that vision of manhood. If you can plant that vision in your heart and begin to pursue it, I'm absolutely certain that you will feel not only more sure about the kind of battles to fight and the kind of battles to avoid, but also an awareness that there is something happening in your life that's good, that you are headed in a direction that is noble and honorable. As you do that, I believe you will experience a sense of dignity that will strengthen your heart and cause your life to really work.

Another translation of Proverbs 29:18 says this: "Where there is no vision [no redemptive revelation of God] the people perish…"[2] I want to help you grasp a redemptive revelation of God so that you come to understand what God expects of you and wants to accomplish in your life. The Bible says that if you can see that vision and follow it, you won't perish; instead, you will make progress. That prophetic vision will set you on the path from *good* man to *valiant* man.

---

2   Proverbs 29:18, AMP

Men are called to follow the example of Jesus

My friend, Jesus Christ is that vision of manhood. If you are a man, then you are called to follow him. He is the ideal Man. In fact, he is the *perfect* Man. In him we have found our true image of manhood. When you and I follow Jesus, we have the privilege of seeing manhood in a most extraordinary and wonderful form. With Jesus you see God in a human body – yet for all the fact that he was God in a human body that body was subject to sexual pressures just like yours. In fact, the Bible says that he was tempted at every point, just as we are tempted.[3] That body had all the same hormones you have, all the same body parts, all the same inward drives, went through puberty, and felt all the pressure of a normal sex drive. Yet, he never once looked at a woman dishonorably or reached out his hand and touched a woman in a way that would dishonor her. He was tempted in every way, just as you are tempted, yet he was without sin.

Hebrews 4:15-16 says:

For we do not have a high priest who is unable to sympathize with our weaknesses, but we have one who has been tempted in every way, just as we are—yet was without sin. Let us then approach the throne of grace with confidence, so that we may receive mercy and find grace to help us in our time of need.

The Bible says that in Jesus we have a High Priest who is able to sympathize with our weaknesses. That means that you and I can approach him with confidence, knowing that He offers us grace to help us in our time of need.

The fact that Jesus never sinned is not a line in the sand intended to increase your level of shame. His perfection is not meant to cast

---

3   Hebrews 4:15

shadows of failure over you. His sinlessness means that you can approach the throne of grace in confidence, knowing that Jesus has been where you are. He knows from experience the struggles men face every day. This fact alone gives you the ability to face even the biggest struggles in life. You may feel that you have the deadliest, darkest secrets any man has ever kept, but you will find that God is close enough to help you when you need his help the most.

In this book I am going to help you to tackle the issue of your sexuality. This is not about stacking up rules to the heavens and making bold and extraordinary promises that you will never again do the wrong thing. This is not about trying harder than you have ever tried before. I'm going to explain things to you about masculinity you have probably never heard before. Together we are going to bust the ignorance barrier and what I have to tell you will help you. I'm going to share skills with you that are essential to you becoming a *valiant man*, and if you are willing to apply them life will be better.

Throughout this book you will feel moments of encouragement and enthusiasm as you understand things you've never understood before and learn skills you've never learned before. These insights and skills will help, but there are some changes that cannot occur in your life without help from a Holy power beyond yourself. I hope to help you to connect with God. I hope to take you on a journey with eternal consequences. You are not reading this book for a simple boost of encouragement. You have picked up this book for a new life, so make a decision right now that you are going to treat the experience like a journey and take on one page after another until you've done the whole trip. I want you to break through the tape at the end of the race knowing that you actually grew throughout the pages of this book.

My friend, this really matters to God! If there is anything that

I am excited about, it is this: I am convinced that as you progress through this book with sincerity and an open heart, that God will join with you in transforming you into a man after His own heart—a *valiant man*. You see, God is *for* you! Jesus is on your side, because what you are pursuing is a high priority to God. As you begin your journey in the pursuit of personal purity you are not alone. You are not reading this book as a Robinson Crusoe. You are taking this journey with thousands of other men who are in a common struggle together: bringing their libido under the Lordship of Christ. Let's go!

CHAPTER 1

BECOMING A REAL MAN

"Men of genius are admired, men of wealth are envied, men of power are feared; but only men of character are trusted."
Source Unknown

"It is not what he had, or even what he does which expresses the worth of a man, but what he is."
Henri Frederic Amiel

A man is called to fulfill many roles: husband, father, son, brother, uncle, grandfather... There's also lover, leader, protector and provider. And each role demands different qualities of us. It seems as if our family and our society continually place demands on men that stretch us to snapping point... all to meet the many challenges of manhood.

Manhood is a multi-faceted calling. The life of Jesus exemplifies the multi-faceted life that you and I, as men, are called to embrace. It was my good friend Rick Yeatts who first introduced me to this concept in an extraordinary message on the Beasts with Four Faces that are referred to in the Bible. It provided me with a vision of manhood I've never forgotten. Who ever heard of a creature that had four faces? In a number of the extraordinary visions of heavenly beings recorded in the Bible these powerful creatures with four faces make an appearance. Rick taught that the four faces were an insight into the perfection of Jesus' manhood and of the manhood that you and I need to embrace. They typify the multi-faceted character that God wants every man to embrace. A man is not intended to be a two-dimensional cardboard cut-out. A man has many different roles and responsibilities. I love these four faces because they exemplify the full canvas of the manhood of Jesus and they provide us with a true, prophetic vision of the kind of man that you and I can become.

The face of an ox

First, there is the face of an ox. This face shows us that God created a man to be a hard worker, to carry burdens. This is one of the reasons why you have more muscle than a woman. As we will unfold in greater detail later in this book, the hormone Testosterone is the defining masculine hormone. Testosterone is responsible for a man's superior muscular development. At his peak physical condition about 40% of a man's body is made up of muscle, whereas only about 23% of a woman's body is muscle. Why is that? It's because a woman is not designed to be an ox. That is a man's role, and that's why he has the physique for it.

Every now and again you hear a man complaining, "Why do I have to mow the lawn? Why won't she go out and do it?" I'll tell you why: because you are the one called to be an ox. That also means going out and changing the oil in the car. You may complain and ask, "Why can't she change the oil in the car for once?" Well, she's not designed to be an ox—you are! One of the reasons why men perform hard work, why men mow lawns, change the tires on the car, start chainsaws, and carry the shopping bags is not because we're crazy, it's because we are designed to be like an ox. It's a grand celebration when a man accepts that one of his roles in life is to be an ox. You are an ox, and you are designed and called to carry burdens, your own and those of others. Get a redemptive revelation of who you are. Accept the call to work hard, to labor and to serve. For the sake of your household, for the sake of your God, and for the sake of your nation, you are called to be a strong ox.

The face of a lion

The second face is that of a lion. This speaks of a man's calling to be bold, to be a protector, to be kingly, to rule, and to take the lead. A husband is called the "head" of his wife. We'll visit this idea again later in the book because it's a vital issue that needs to be understood rightly. To be like a lion does not mean that men should be bossy, but it does embrace the fact that God put within us this testosterone-driven system to be bold, to be active, to be proactive, to have a go, to be brave, and to lead. We are to take on our challenges like a lion.

The Bible says: "The righteous are as bold as a lion."[4] Boldness is part of what men are called to be. Now, you will need to recognize that you can't be bold about everything and you can't be bold all the time. Remember that some of the time you are to be like an ox, and at other times you are to exercise your role as a lion—protecting your wife and children, protecting things that matter in your community and in your nation, taking up the challenge to be a bold knight in shining armor. Get a redemptive vision of your call to be a lion; this is part of what a man is called to be.

The face of an eagle

The third face is that of an eagle. This is the recognition that a man is called to be spiritual, to mount up on wings like eagles[5], to ascend to the throne room of God in worship and prayer, and develop great faith in God. It's interesting to note that in the Bible this face was not the face that was presented to others. This face was the face behind. We are not supposed to be trying to show our spiritual face everywhere we go. Often our prayer is in secret, and our fasting is in secret, and our giving is in secret, but this spiritual face is at the back of everything we do and everything we are. It is the desire of God that every man would have the sense that he can become a prayer warrior for his family, that he can become an example of a worshipper to his family, that he can become a man of God. The face of an eagle means that you are not just called to carry burdens, you are not just called to be a knight in shining armor; you are also called to be a spiritual man. Get a redemptive revelation of your calling as an eagle. You are called to be a godly

---

4   Proverbs 28:1
5   Isaiah 40:31, KJV

man, a man of prayer, worship and spiritual authority who knows how to stand in his presence.

The face of a man

The last face is the face of a man. This is the face that the Beasts presented as the face in front. It is a part of your calling to learn to handle your humanity well. God designed you within a human frame. He designed you with a nervous system. He designed you with hormones. You have a man's sexual system. You have a man's sexual make-up. You have a man's sex drive. It will do you well to never forget that. Clinical psychologist Dr. Archibald Hart said about Christian ministers who get into moral strife, *"Ministers don't fall because they forget they're Christians, they fall because they forget they're men."* They forget they have hormones. They forget they have a sex drive. They forget they are not just an eagle, an ox and a lion—they are also human. The fact is that you are a man, not a superman. You are not a god or an angel. You need to recognize that as you live out your calling as an ox, as a lion, and as an eagle, you do it in the frame of a man.

One of the reasons why men pick up this book or enroll in a Valiant Man program is that they want to understand who they are as a man. They want to understand why they sometimes feel the way they do. They want to understand how a man's sex drive actually works. They want to understand what it is that can twist a man's sex drive out of shape. They want to understand the frailties and the limitations of their humanity so that they don't destroy themselves.

In Genesis 2:15 the Creator lays out Adam's job description in the Garden of Eden: "The Lord God took the man and put him in the Garden of Eden to work it and take care of it." Here God was giving the man a sphere of responsibility. He said to Adam, "I want you to work it and take care of it." In this passage of Scripture there are two key Hebrew words: *abad* and *shamar*. *Abad* means "to work", "to labor" and "to serve". The word *abad* correlates to the calling of an ox. You and I are called to work, we are called to labor, and we are called to serve. At the same time, a man is called to *shamar*, which means "to guard", "to keep" and "to protect". The word *shamar* correlates to the calling of a lion. You are called to be a defender of your household.

Now here's the deal: If your sexuality is distorted and out of control, you will never guard, keep and protect those you love. Sadly, when a man's sexuality is distorted, women and children tend to pay the price. God did not call us to be predators. God didn't call us to wound or use those he has put under our care. He has asked us to lift them up and to protect them. So we must learn how to work for, labor on behalf of and serve our families. We must learn how to guard, keep and protect them. One of the profound gifts that you can give your family is to be a man of sexual purity, to be a man whose life is really under control. That, my friend, must be your goal.

The *valiant man* understands that he is not primarily called to be a taker. Instead, he is primarily called to give. It is one of the most important insights for us to understand. You were born a man, which means that if you are a husband, then you are the head of your wife.[6] Don't quickly pass over this point. What does it mean to be the head of your wife? What does it mean for a man to say "I'm the head." Does that mean you get to decide how to spend all the money? Does that mean you get to sign all the checks? Does that mean you get to own the remote controls in the home?

6   Ephesians 5:23

Does that mean you get to say where the family goes on holidays? Does that mean you get to make all the decisions and tell everyone what to do? No, that's not what headship is all about. The tragedy is when a man does not understand that God gave him strength, boldness and vitality to serve others, then he starts to think that headship is about being in charge, being the boss, getting to run and rule everything. But that is not the essence of headship.

Real Headship

The Bible says about our headship, "Husbands, love your wives, just as Christ loved the church and gave himself up for her."[7] In other words, Jesus was saying, "You get to be the head of your wife like I'm the Head of the Church." The same friend who told me about the beasts with four faces also had this to say about headship: "Headship means that you get to die first." I rate it as one of the most significant insights I have ever heard. It changed forever my understanding of headship. That's what Jesus did for his bride, the church. Jesus did not arrive in some kind of four-wheeled golden pumpkin, park in the middle of the city square, throw on a purple robe, sit on His throne and declare, "Right, everybody, here I am! I'm the King of kings. I'm the head. I'm in charge. Everybody come and serve me!" Instead, Jesus turned up on this earth in a stable full of animals. He then chose to lay his life down and perish for his bride, the church. Then he rose again for her, and has been living ever since to teach her and caress her, to nurture her and strengthen her, so that she gets to make it into eternal life. He died first.

Jesus says to every man, "You get to be the head of your home like I'm the head of the church." A *valiant man* understands headship.

---

7   Ephesians 5:25

He realizes that the health of his family begins with him, that the moral strength of his family begins with him, that the security of his family begins with him, and that the emotional health of his family begins with him. It isn't the children's responsibility to take the first steps of discipleship to establish a healthy home. It's not your wife's responsibility to make it all happen. If you want to be a valiant man, then you get to die first, because you are the head, and headship means that the quality of your family's life begins with you.

The *valiant man* understands that responsibility. He understands the true nature of headship. He understands that he is called to serve. He understands that the future of his family is profoundly impacted by his own growth, his own walk with God, his own personal maturity. He understands that he is the one who gets to go to battle for them. He understands that he first deals with himself and his passions for the sake of his wife, his children, his church and his nation.

How central is the issue of sexual purity?

In the journey from *good* man to *valiant* man, sexual purity is a core issue. If you've read the Old Testament you could be confused about that. For instance, David had six wives, Solomon had a harem, and Abraham didn't mind handing his wife over to another man when the pressure was on. In fact, the Old Testament characters are a mixed bag when it comes to the issue of sexual purity. Yet when you read the New Testament, the story takes a dramatic turn.

When the church first started and people began to come to Jesus, it was largely made up of Jewish believers. As more and more Gentiles came to Christ, the question was asked: "How much of the Old Testament are we supposed to make these new believers obey?" Some were saying all new believers should be required to embrace the whole Old Testament religious system while others were saying it was a new day and a new way. So they held a meeting in Jerusalem to try to figure out what to tell these new, non-Jewish believers. When they finally resolved the issue, they only came up with four key instructions. Moses had Ten Commandments, but the elders in the Early Church only came up with four. This is what they had to say:

> For it has seemed good to the Holy Spirit and to us to lay on you no greater burden than these requirements: that you abstain from what has been sacrificed to idols, and from blood, and from what has been strangled, and from sexual immorality. If you keep yourselves from these, you will do well.[8]

The first three instructions were cultural issues largely related to the fact that in the first century everybody was connected to a temple of some kind erected to the worship of some deity or another. The temples functioned both as places of worship and as restaurants where the sacrificial meal was cooked and eaten with friends. The intention of those first three instructions was simply this: If you have come to see Jesus as the only one worthy of worship, your old temple affiliations are over. However, the fourth issue—about sexual immorality—goes way beyond being a cultural issue. In effect, those early church elders were saying: "If you want to do well in your walk with God, you just have to clean up your sex life." The same applies today. If you and I, as men, do not rise above the tide of sexual immorality that is seeping through our world, we will not do well. But if we do—if you and I can become *valiant men*—we will do well.

---

8   Acts 15:28-29

Later in the New Testament the Apostle Paul explains in greater detail what that instruction about abstaining from sexual immorality means. In 1 Thessalonians chapter 4, talking about that instruction he says, "Finally, then, brothers, we ask and urge you in the Lord Jesus, that as you received from us how you ought to walk and to please God, just as you are doing, that you do so more and more."[9]

This demonstrates that sexual purity is not just about outward behavior, it's also about an increasing purity of thought and motivation. If this was just about sexual behavior, such as don't commit adultery and don't fornicate, then you would hardly be asked by the Apostle Paul to do that "more and more", would you?! You are either doing it or you are not doing it! No, what Paul was saying here is this: "When I came to you (Thessalonians) and I said to you that we are going to abstain from sexual immorality, I'm so proud of you guys because you took it seriously, and you changed some of your behaviors. But now I'm going to encourage you to go beyond behaviors to thoughts and the passions of your heart. I'm going to encourage you to now consider the secret life on the inside. I'm going to encourage you to take that purity and extend it more and more."

Sexual purity is progressive

My friend, this is great news because it underlines to us that purity is a progressive process. It means that nobody can just make a decision to suddenly be pure. You can't simply say to me, "Al, I'm moved by what you are saying and I want to be a valiant man, so I promise that I will be a pure man from now on." The fact is that it wouldn't be possible for you to keep that promise, because

9   1 Thessalonians 4:1, ESV

purity is not just about not fornicating with somebody, it's not just about abstaining from adultery, it's not even just about cutting out masturbation. You see, it extends to the thoughts of a man, to the desires that drive him and the preoccupation of his mind.

Purity is a battle that is won progressively. You cannot make a decision today and say, "I will be pure for the rest of my life!" You and I don't have the skills or the ability to do that. It would be like saying to a five-year-old, "I want you to qualify for the Olympic high jump, so make a decision now to achieve that goal!" So the child runs down the athletic track and jumps over the bar at two feet. He runs and jumps again, but it doesn't matter how hard he tries or how committed he is, he does not have the development to get him over the two meter qualifying height. That is what purity is like. Purity means to be pure like Jesus, to never look at a woman with lust, to never touch a woman with evil intent, to have your heart clean and untainted despite the pressure of temptation. That's a significant challenge—and you may already feel that it will forever be beyond you.

However, it is my conviction that as you progress through this book, you will grow in strength and in the ability to manage your life. You are going to learn skills about your thought life, about your eyes, about your speech and about your passions. You are going to discover how these cycles start within you and where they will carry you if you let them. I am going to help you unpick some of damage of the past, so that the time will come when you will be able to look back and say, "I'm not perfect yet, but I'm not like I used to be!"

The issue of your purity is a matter of great importance. It matters to God that we take our purity seriously. The Apostle Paul goes on to say:

> For you know what instructions we gave you through the Lord Jesus.
> For this is the will of God, your sanctification: that you abstain from
> sexual immorality; that each one of you know how to control his

own body in holiness and honor [*so there is some self control involved*], not in the passion of lust like the Gentiles who do not know God; that no one transgress and wrong his brother in this matter, because the Lord is an avenger in all these things, as we told you beforehand and solemnly warned you. For God has not called us for impurity, but in holiness. Therefore whoever disregards this, disregards not man but God, who gives his Holy Spirit to you.[10]

Why is male sexuality so prone to distortions?

I was a self-taught golfer. I learned the hard way that when you try to teach yourself a complex skill you can groove in some pretty unhelpful distortions. I had a passion to play golf well enough to break par, but no matter how hard I tried it was an elusive dream. I was playing golf with our club professional one day when he said to a friend of mine, "It's a pity about Al. He'll never break par with that swing." When I heard what he'd said I decided to sign up for lessons and get the swing I needed. The pro took me right back to basics and rebuilt my swing; the grip, back swing, stance, firing order, snap – the whole thing. He taught me how to control my body. During the learning process I got worse before I got better. In fact, for three months I was so bad I couldn't hit myself in the foot! But then one glorious day, after three months of frustrating practice, the new swing came in. I thought I'd died and gone to heaven. Since that time my best round in competition is two under par. Trying hard was not enough—I needed lessons.

The passage above says we are called to control our own body, not to be ruled by passion and lust. We have all been subject to

---

10   1 Thessalonians 4:2-8, ESV

distortions in our sexuality, and those distortions are the result of numerous pressures in our lives. Just like my golf swing, trying hard will not be enough to restore or fortify your moral and spiritual character. When it came to my golf swing I was unable to teach myself how to control that body of mine. Left to yourself you may never learn how to control your libido, so I'm going to teach you how. Throughout this book you and I are going to take a look at these various pressures that may have distorted your sexuality, and I am going to teach you the skills necessary to make the progress that will take you from *good* man to *valiant man.*

For instance, I can guarantee that most men have no idea how deeply their sexual struggles are related to the fact that man was created for intimacy with God. In this fallen world we don't experience the level of face to face intimacy God created us for, and that loss of experience of being loved, nurtured, and deeply connected with God makes us so vulnerable to our own sexual passions. I'll explain this in greater detail later in this book.

Then there is the issue of the wiring of the male brain. We'll unpack this issue in detail in Chapter 3, but I'm going to help you understand something of the chemistry set inside your head that relates to sexual arousal; understanding that chemistry set will become a key to learning the first skill of the *valiant man*—eye control. Understanding brain function will also become a key to understanding how to go from good to valiant in terms of the *big three*: fantasy, pornography and masturbation.

Another pressure that can distort male sexuality is the power of the male hormonal engine. And it's a very powerful engine indeed! I'll help you to understand how your hormones work, when they start to kick in, and how to manage the relentless sexual pressure they generate.

As men, we need to appreciate the influence that secular standards and values have on our lives. You and I are under immense pressure from the rampant sexualizing and eroticizing of every kind of media which, combined with our hormonal engine, can distort our sexuality to the point of our own destruction. Throughout this book, we'll learn how to respond to that pressure.

The falling age in puberty and the rising age in marriage is another potential source of distortion in our sexuality. In modern society there is, on average, an 18 year gap between the emergence of our sex drive (around 11 or 12 years of age) and the righteous fulfillment of it in a married relationship (now around the age of 30 for men). The potential for distortions to occur during that period of a man's life is significant—and without help he can carry those distortions into his marriage with sad and unhelpful consequences. Every young man entering puberty will need help to handle that pressure; for his own sake and for the sake of the women and children to whom he will later relate.

Then there is the emotional and spiritual fallout that men experience as a result of all the pressures we've already mentioned. Even good men wonder if they are normal. Even good men struggle with intrusive sexual thoughts. Even good men make mistakes and find themselves impacted by their sexuality in ways that causes them to wonder if God would like them, use them or approve of them. There is no question that every man needs help to handle these pressures appropriately. The journey from *good* man to *valiant* man is a journey of profound importance. The stakes are high. We must undertake the journey, and we must succeed.

A lesson from the life of Ezra

There's one more thing I need to say about that journey before we conclude this chapter. There is a man in the Bible who can teach us a thing or two about manhood. He was a priest in Babylon at the end of the Babylonian captivity. Jerusalem had been destroyed some 70 years earlier, and now the time had come to go back and rebuild the devastated city. It was a man named Ezra who, along with a bunch of others, willingly returned to that ruined city and began rebuilding the city walls. Not everyone in captivity made that journey. Not everyone who was in captivity took their opportunity for freedom. In fact, less than 50,000 made that journey back to Jerusalem. The majority never left the land of their captivity in Babylon. Ezra explained the difference between the exiles who returned to rebuild and the exiles that remained in captivity forever: The ones who escaped captivity were those *"whose spirit God had stirred to go up and rebuild the house of the Lord which is in Jerusalem."* (Ezra 1:5)

The lesson you and I can learn from this story is this: We will not accomplish the rebuilding of our moral walls unless the Spirit of God stirs our hearts. It is my prayer that as you read this book you will allow God's Spirit to stir you to action in this strengthening and rebuilding process. If you approach this process somewhat reluctantly or casually you may remain a captive forever. To see real and lasting change in your life, you must approach this book declaring, *I have to do this journey! I have to go down this pathway! I need to rebuild the walls in my life! I need to fortify myself and strengthen my soul!* Only those whose hearts are stirred by God will grow from *good* to *valiant* on this journey, and there is something you can do to posture yourself for divine help along the way. Here it is:

The vital starting point

Ezra only took those with him who were stirred in their heart and willing to have a crack at the rebuilding process. So back to Jerusalem they went. The city was ruined and the walls had been torn down. Yet they didn't make the rebuilding of the walls their first priority. What is so important about this story is what they *did* make their highest priority.

Ezra walked past the fallen walls, through the burned down gates, through the ruined city, until he stood in front of the spot where the temple had once stood. Then they scratched around in the rubble until they discovered the foundation of the old altar where 70-odd years before the morning and evening sacrifices had been made to the Lord. When they had cleared away the rubble, they began to rebuild that altar. When they had finally restored it, they began the morning and evening sacrifices once again.[11] The altar was their first priority, and it was the right priority.

The significance here for you and me is that before they attempted to rebuild that city, they found the altar and restored morning and evening worship. What Ezra and his men were saying, in effect, was this: "We are not going to be able to pull this off in our own strength. We are not going to be able to protect ourselves on our own. We first and foremost need you, God!"

Now, I don't know to what degree you need to rebuild your life, my friend. I guarantee there is not one man reading this book whose walls are perfect and whose entire life is safe and totally under control. Even though the city's walls were shattered and Ezra and his group were vulnerable to attack from neighboring nations, Ezra and his men didn't begin their task by trying to do appearance management or make bold promises about the construction time-frame. They didn't hold a management meeting and say, "Okay, let's try to put things in order as fast as we can and then defend ourselves." No, they left the walls lying broken and shattered as they first went to the altar. They simply said to God, "Here we are.

---

11   Ezra 3:3

We're back again. We need you. And if you don't help us, we will never get this job done." Your personal disciplines and concentration will be important, but they are not the highest priority. You won't become a *valiant man* just by trying really, really hard. You need help that comes from outside yourself.

That's why, over the course of this book, I'm going to invite you to do the same thing. Every morning and every evening bring your journey before God in worship and prayer. Get hold of the Valiant Man Daily Journal[12], because as you read it each morning and each evening it will help you to bring your life back to the altar of God and say to him, "Here I am, God! Help me! You know me better than I know myself, and I trust you to help me." It's not going to require a lot of time and it's not going to be very complex, but it will change your life completely. Like Ezra and his men, your first priority should be to meet with God in a moment of devotion, prayer and quiet reflection each morning and evening.

"What if I don't believe in God?" you may ask. "I'm just not really sure who God is," you may be saying. My friend, you may not have a clue if there even is a God! Well, I'll tell you what you should do: conduct a scientific experiment. Herbert Spencer, one of the key originators of Alcoholics Anonymous literature, once stated: "There is a principle which is a bar against all information, which is proof against all arguments, and which cannot fail to keep a man in everlasting ignorance. That principle is contempt prior to investigation."[13] As Herbert Spencer has suggested, why don't you investigate the possibility of divine love and help before you dismiss it contemptuously. Rather than despising the idea before investigation, rather than barring the idea of God from your thought life, conduct an experiment and simply say this, *If there's nothing out*

---

12   www.careforcelifekeys.org
13   Herbert Spencer, quoted from Alcoholics Anonymous, pages 569-570.

there, opening myself to nothing can't hurt me. So I can't be a loser for simply having an open mind about this whole thing.

Then conduct this experiment: Get your hands on the *Valiant Man Daily Journal* and open your mind and your heart to a time of reflection morning and evening—and see what happens in your life. If nothing happens, you haven't lost anything—but at least you had a go.

However, what if for some reason, in the midst of reading through this book and the *Valiant Man Daily Journal*, wisdom comes to you that you never anticipated? What if strength or healing should come to an area of your life that you never expected and you cannot explain? At that point, would you be willing to say, "Well that was amazing! Whoever did that, thank you very much!" If you have the integrity and willingness of heart to conduct an experiment like that, whether you believe in God or not, I think you will find that God will respond. The Bible says, "Taste and see that the Lord is good."[14] It is my conviction that God, who loves you so much, will reach through your honesty and your openness and reveal himself to you.

When that happens, I invite you to simply pray this prayer:
"Lord, guide me as I begin this journey of discovery. Change me
and help me to grow. Make me a valiant man."

---

14   Psalm 34:8

REFLECTION

Pause right now to consider what kind of a man you want to be. Does the vision for manhood that I have outlined in this chapter capture your heart?

It is my hope and my prayer that you will embrace the vision to become a man who knows how to carry his responsibility, a man who knows how to be brave and to stand up for those whom he loves, a man who knows how to rise up in the presence of God and touch the face of God, but also a man who understands his own weaknesses, his own frailties and his own humanity.

That's a magnificent journey and a grand goal, my friend. And I believe that you and I can do it together as we leaf through the pages of this book.

CHAPTER 2

THE RIGHT ATTITUDES

"Human beings, by changing the inner attitudes of their
minds, can change the outer aspects of their lives."
William James

"A strong positive mental attitude will create more miracles
than any wonder drug."
Patricia Neal

I love the brand of football known as Australian Rules football, or Aussie Rules – the oldest football code in the world. If you aren't familiar with Aussie Rules, it's a game played on a huge arena about 200 yards from end to end (I still don't think in meters!) and it's just as wide. There's a lot of grass out there! It's an amazing spectacle to watch 36 super athletes run onto the ground in their sleeveless jumpers, shorts, long socks and footy boots, and play their hearts out for two solid hours of bone-jarring, heart-stopping contest. No helmets or padding—just bare arms and legs, guts, speed and determination; and when those guys run across that white boundary line and onto that arena you know you're about to see one of the greatest sporting spectacles in the world.

One thing you can almost guarantee at an Aussie Rules match is a huge crowd. Sometimes the crowd is as much a spectacle as the game itself. In fact, I've noticed something funny about specta-tors—they make way more noise than the players, they never drop the ball, they never miss a kick for goal, they know way more about the game than the umpires; and when the siren finally sounds at the end of the match, you can hear half of them screaming, "We won! We won!" The strange thing is that they were never in the game! They should be screaming, "We watched! We watched!" Only the guys down in the arena were actually in the game. For all the noise they made, the rest were nothing but spectators. How would you like to stop being a spectator and get into the real game of life on the Arena of Healing?

Jesus Christ is the greatest healer and teacher the world has ever known. All of Western Civilization today lives in the blessing of the truth that he taught while on this earth. The best elements of our society have been structured around the ideas, the concepts and the values that Jesus Christ delivered to us. In one extraordinary teaching session Jesus spelled out eight attitudes that are absolutely crucial to success, restoration and healing in life. If you are willing to stop being a spectator, if you are willing to get out of the grandstand and into the arena of healing, if you want to quit feeling helpless watching other people kick goals, Jesus Christ can explain to you how to get over the boundary line and into the game so that you can actually kick some goals yourself.

That sermon is called the Sermon on the Mount[15]. Jesus was doing some great things at that time. He was healing the sick, raising the dead, and curing people who were insane. Huge crowds were gathering to hear him and bringing sick and needy people from all the surrounding regions for healing. Jesus was demonstrating what the power of God can do in a needy human life, but on this particular day he stopped the healing and took his disciples aside for some instruction. It was as if he was saying to them, "Hey, fellas. I've got some good news and I've got some bad news. Do you want to hear the good news? Here's the good news: People can receive blessing. The Kingdom of God is incredibly powerful and if a human life connects with God's grace and God's love, that life is going to be blessed and favored. That's the good news. Once you connect with God, things can change and become healthy. But here's the bad news: Not everybody is going to make that connection. I'll tell you why—because making that connection requires that you adopt certain attitudes, that you posture yourself in a certain way, that you react in a certain way to the challenges of life. Blessed are the poor in spirit, for the Kingdom of God will be theirs."

What does it mean to be *blessed*?

The word *blessing* is a very powerful word. It's a word that is used quite frequently in the Bible. In fact, it is one of the first words

---

15   Matthew 5:2-9

you hear in the Bible. Right up the front of the Book, in Genesis, the Bible says, "And God blessed them, and God said unto them, 'Be fruitful, and multiply, and replenish the earth...'"[16] Here we see that God's blessing is his power conferred on a human life—power to fulfill one's destiny and to succeed in one's calling in life. That's what it means to be *blessed*..

The word *blessed* means "favored by God" and "empowered to succeed". God says to you, "I want you to make it! I want you to succeed! I want you to experience real life!" And when God blesses a life, it's as if he puts His hands on both shoulders and says, "I'm going to give you the power to succeed." Now that's good news, my friend! That's good news for *you* as you travel this journey towards personal purity, towards becoming a *valiant man*, towards learning to become the ox, the lion, the eagle and the man that God created you to be.

In your journey from good man to valiant man, you don't have to go it alone—the blessing can be yours; you can be empowered by God to succeed. However, to be empowered by that blessing you will need to be willing to embrace certain attitudes. The greatest healer in the world spelled out eight life-changing attitudes that you will need to adopt if you want to succeed in life and if you want to experience the healing of your manhood. If you adopt them, you will find the power to succeed and to be healed. If you don't adopt these attitudes, no matter how much you say you'd like to succeed and change and become a *valiant man*, you're on your own. You can read this book and even attend all the Valiant Man programs, small groups and group discussions, but if you don't adopt these key attitudes, you will encounter no more success than you can

16   Genesis 1:28

muster on your own. Would you like to know the attitudes you must embrace to encounter God's power filled blessing? Hold on to your hat, here they come:

Attitude 1: Humility (the poor in spirit)

Blessed are the poor in spirit,
for theirs is the kingdom of heaven.[17]

The first attitude is humility. When a man embraces the attitude of humility, he climbs down out of the grandstand and takes his first step over the boundary line and onto the arena of healing. God resists the proud but he has grace for the humble. Humility qualifies you for his blessing: the power to succeed in becoming a *valiant man*.

This is what the attitude of humility sounds like:

I am not a perfect man. I recognize that I have deficiencies, weaknesses, and brokenness within myself which impact my sexuality and I am incapable of rectifying them in my own strength. I need help.

Perhaps the greatest enemy to any man making progress towards becoming a *valiant man* is the issue of denial. Denial says to self and to others, "You know, I don't have a real problem here, mate. It's not that serious. I'll be right, buddy. No problems. No worries. No big deal." Denial says, "I don't want to face my problems." Denial flows from a fear of acknowledging the truth about your life. Denial doesn't want to notice the problem, the seriousness of the situation, or how unpleasant the reality of your life actually is.

---

17   Matthew 5:3

There is a tendency in humanity to simply pretend not to notice problems. Sergeant Shultz on the old T.V. program Hogan's Heroes would regularly proclaim "I see nothing, I see nothing." Your marriage may be falling apart, your health may be deteriorating, it might be obvious that your life is on a downward spiral, and yet there may be a reluctance to acknowledge the unpleasant realities and ask for help. That's denial, my friend.

The courage to face our problems

One of the great marks of God's grace and love at work in a man's life is when he begins to have the courage to face what is really happening in his life. It is a mark of God's grace when denial is pierced and humility begins its precious work. The reality for all of us is that we don't want to think of ourselves as addicts in any way. One of the hardest things for a person facing alcohol addiction is to be able to say, "My life has become unmanageable and I have to confess I am powerless against alcohol." The problem may have been of crisis proportions for years, yet denial will still say, "I can handle it. I can stop whenever I want. I have stopped thousands of times before and I know I can do it again." It's the same for any addiction. People have said that about smoking. "I haven't got a problem with smoking," they say. "I've stopped hundreds of times. I can do it any time I want."

You cannot change what you will not acknowledge. If you have difficulty thinking of yourself as an addict or as someone on the road to addiction, then that denial will make it difficult for you to make the progress that you need to make, especially if it is a sexual addiction. That's why humility is the place to begin the journey towards healing.

If you have a religious background, finding the humility to confront the issue of moral purity can be more difficult than for those who have no religious principles. Research shows that people with religious backgrounds see sexual struggles as much more shameful than either addiction to cigarettes or addiction to gambling. On the other hand, irreligious people will have a tendency to view private sexual behavior as a non-issue. "Who cares!" they may say. "So what if I masturbate and watch pornography! What's the big deal if I live with my head in that space?"

Having a religious background increases the tendency to see sexual problems as more shameful than gambling problems or drug addiction. If you've had a religious background it would probably be easier to confess that you have a problem with gambling than to confess to a problem with masturbation. There is such potential for feelings of shame around the issue of sex. It is such a private, personal issue that the potential for denial is very strong. Humility may not be easy. It will take great courage, but it will be well rewarded.

Understanding the road towards sexual addiction

Addiction is a word that is used very loosely in our culture. People talk about being addicted to chocolate, addicted to their mobile phone, even addicted to exercise—although I've never felt much in danger of that one! Later in this book we will explore the issue of addiction in greater detail, and I'll provide a more clinically accurate definition of addiction in general and sexual addiction in particular. At this point let's remain non-technical and describe an addiction simply as: Going far enough down a pathway of behavior in any area of life to find that the behavior persists to your own detriment, the detriment of others, and against your own better judgment.

Jesus is the example of a *valiant man* with a perfectly pure heart.

Purity is home base for the *valiant man*. There is a proverb that states, "A journey of a thousand miles begins with one step." That's how it is with sexual addiction. One step away from purity is a step on the road towards sexual addiction. The road to addiction is paved with steps that were small, inappropriate responses to an appetite or desire. It's not sexual addiction because you enjoy sex. And it's not sexual addiction because you have a lot of sex. It's the demand for sex and the demand for pleasure that result in cumulative, inappropriate steps away from purity which leads to the painful reality of sexual addiction.

Let me explain. In their book *Every Man's Battle*, Stephen Arterburn and Fred Stoeker use a very useful term; they talk about *fractional addiction*. It's not easy for a man to see his struggles with sex, pornography, or masturbation as being in the category of an addiction. It is natural to want to minimize the problem, to excuse the struggle as a bit of a challenge but nothing to ring alarm bells over. It would be rare for any man to quickly confess, "Well, yeah, I'm an addict." Many of us reading this book may not even meet all the criteria for Patrick Carnes description of a level one addiction, but I guarantee every one of us has been impacted in our sexuality to the point that we have departed from the purity Jesus exhibited. We would have to acknowledge that we are not pure like Jesus was pure. We have departed from a state of sexual purity and we have made some steps down the road towards impurity, a road that at some point arrives at a destination you could only describe as sexual addiction. That's what Arterburn and Stoeker call *fractional addiction*.

Now, you may not consider yourself to be an addict and by any reasonable definition of the term "addiction" you may not be one. "I'm not in the grip of pornography," you may say. "I don't find myself buying pornographic material every week. I don't find myself regularly looking at it or downloading it on the internet.

No, I'm not at that level." Well, the truth may be that from time to time you feel the pressure of pornography and resist it, but just occasionally you yield to it. You may feel that on a scale of one to ten you're not even a level one addict, but if you're honest you have to acknowledge, "I've moved some way from being as pure as Jesus." If that's you, then you need to humbly acknowledge that your *fractional addiction* needs to be addressed. My friend, you will never change what you will not acknowledge.

When I was a young high school teacher, sexual thoughts were so intrusive in my mind I found it distressing at times. I remember standing in one keyboard class silently crying out to God, *I feel like I'm going insane!* My thoughts were all too regularly filled with sexual pressure. I had only just started to become a serious Christian at that time, and those intrusive thoughts distressed me. I remember walking up and down the classrooms, teaching the students, but at the same time I was crying out to God, *God, it's like I'm living in a hell where I don't know how to stop these rampant, pressing thoughts occupying my mind!* I was struggling with fractional addiction. I've since discovered that even *good* men face this battle.

The truth is that every man is not a sex addict, but every man is under pressure to move in that direction. That's why I've written this book and that's why you're reading it. You need to ask yourself, *How far have I been moved down that pathway of impurity?*

It will require humility to answer that question truthfully, and if you don't answer it truthfully you simply can't change. That's why the greatest Healer that ever walked this earth said this: "Do you want the power to succeed? Blessed are the broken, for theirs is the Kingdom of heaven." Do you want the power of God? Well, then, you are going to need to express humility, and you are going to need to face your challenges as they really are. Humility is the first step in your journey from *good* man to *valiant* man.

Attitude 2: Emotional honesty (those who mourn)

Blessed are those who mourn,
for they will be comforted.[18]

Jesus, the greatest healer the world has ever known, also said this: "Do you want the power to succeed? Well, blessed are those who mourn." Here Jesus is referring to emotional honesty. Jesus said, "If you embrace humility and face reality, you must also face the *feelings* that come with it." Sometimes that will mean feeling grief and disappointment. That's reality, my friend.

Emotional honesty says:

I will no longer deny, ignore or repress my emotional pain. I will weep my tears, groan my groans, cry my cries, and grieve my grief. My emotions are indicators of my heart's condition and I will admit to them freely.

There have been times in my walk with my wife and with my God in which I have felt overwhelmed by the intensity of my personal struggles. In 1981 I was in full-time ministry and I found myself deeply attracted to another woman. For a whole year those feelings would not go away. There were times when I was so distressed because of the relentless struggle I just put my head down on a table and cried like a baby. I wept my heart out. I cried out to God: "How can I be like this?"

Psalm 34 tells us, "This poor man cried, and the Lord heard him and saved him out of all his troubles."[19] I have felt the intensity of my struggle, and as I have cried out to God, He has heard me and delivered me. One of the reasons why I am qualified to write this

18   Matthew 5:4
19   Psalm 34:6, ESV

book is that I am a survivor. I have felt the pressures and I have come through. But I have taken the pressures to the right place, and that is why I am still standing, and that is why I am encouraged to help lead you down a pathway to become a *valiant man.*

The enemies of the healing process in your life are denial, repressed emotions and appearance management. It's time for emotional honesty.

Psychologist Dr. Archibald Hart says that after years of research into men's sexual issues, the statistics show that most men wonder if they are normal. His research was with good men— men in ministry and men training for the ministry, men who loved God and wanted to serve Christ and their community. Dr. Hart discovered that most men—even *good* men—feel a level of distress about the intensity and sometimes the inappropriateness of their sexual passions, desires, feelings, thoughts and even their behaviors. My friend, you need to know that you are not alone.

Be prepared to grieve the grief, cry the cries, and feel the feelings. In the *Valiant Man Daily Journal* there are sections left blank where a man can write about his feelings. If you have the Journal, you may want to write: *I feel hopeless and I think I need help!* You need to be honest like that. The poor man described in Psalm 34 cried out and the Lord heard him and delivered him out of all of his distress. Jesus said, "Blessed are those who mourn, for they will be comforted."[20]

Now, if you want to continue with appearance management— pretending everything is fine and putting up a false front—you can, but in doing so you have chosen not to step into the arena of healing. You're not even in the game, and the struggle will continue, perhaps for the rest of your life. The power to make progress in

---

20   Matthew 5:4

managing your sexuality well only comes to those who are prepared to cry the cries, groan the groans, grieve the grief, and call on the name of the Lord. So I encourage you to do that.

When a man experiences humility, he begins to face what he really is. When you put humility and emotional honesty together, it results in a wonderful thing called confession. Confession means telling the truth. There is amazing power in breaking the silence, telling the truth to another human being, and having that human being speak affirmation over you, encouraging you that God is for you, that He will forgive you and restore you.

During the Reformation, Martin Luther formalized this into a doctrine that he called 'The Office of the Keys'. In fact, it was based on Jesus' words. After Jesus had risen from the dead he met with his disciples and the Bible says that Jesus "breathed on them and said, 'Receive the Holy Spirit. If you forgive anyone his sins, they are forgiven; if you do not forgive them, they are not forgiven.'"[21] Jesus gave his disciples authority to proclaim forgiveness over people. James, a brother of Jesus, expressed this privilege in these words: "Therefore confess your sins to each other and pray for each other so that you may be healed."[22] That doesn't mean we can go around selling indulgences. It doesn't mean we can go around flippantly saying, "Okay, I forgive you!" But what Jesus conferred on his disciples was the power to hear the confession of another human being and reach out a hand and say, "In Jesus' name, I can proclaim to you that your sins are forgiven."

Confession and forgiveness is such a wonderful, potent and powerful process; make a decision to accept the privilege of being a carrier of the forgiveness of sins to other men. If you are privileged to be trusted with an honest confession, have the courage to

21   John 20:22-23
22   James 5:16

ask, "Can I pray with you?" If you get the opportunity don't hold back. Be bold and gracious, and confer on another the forgiveness of sins in Jesus name. That's one of the privileges that come with confession. Combining humility with emotional honesty opens the door for confession and the forgiveness of sins. In that environment the power of God is available to release from the shame, the guilt and the pressure so often part of a man's sexual development and sexual experience.

Attitude 3: Teachability (the meek)

Blessed are the meek,
for they will inherit the earth.[23]

Meekness is an attitude that takes down the defenses and says, "I am willing to be corrected. I am willing to hear the truth, even if the truth challenges me and shows that I am in need of change." The opposite of meekness is defensiveness. Every one of us could be somewhat further down the road to being healthy, valiant men if we were not so defensive when we face a truth that we find challenging. Because of the shame factor, because of our brokenness, when truth comes to us it sometimes pins us to the wall. When that happens, our tendency is to push it away. Our response may be, "Oh, I don't want to hear that!" Another response may be, "But you don't understand my circumstances."

This is what meekness sounds like:

I will open my heart and mind to receive the truth, even if that truth

---

23   Matthew 5:5

shows me to be guilty of wrong and in need of painful change. I decide not to hide myself from accountability, nor will I shield myself from loving and truthful reflection. With a gentle spirit I will listen to your insights and without being judgmental I will share mine with you.

As men, there is often a desire to fight back when we are confronted with painful, humbling truth. Sometimes that means we shoot the messenger. There is no hope for change if you do not let the truth in. Meekness says, "Tell me the truth. I want to let it in." Jesus said the most important of all his parables was the Parable of the Sower.[24] Jesus used the metaphor of seed to explain the effectiveness and power of truth. In essence Jesus said, "You need to understand that truth is like a seed. No matter how small or simple a truth may seem to be, when truth gets into the human heart it begins to unpack itself, reform behavior, and produce a different life."

Jesus went on to explain that there are four reasons why the truth can't get in. First, truth doesn't find its way into your life because you don't understand it. The pity is that you and I can *decide* not to understand it. Often it's not that we don't really understand it, it's that we don't want to let it in. In our stubborn defiance, we resist the truth. The failure to understand the truth has a consequence. In effect, Jesus said, "If truth comes to you and you act like an idiot, then that truth will be taken away. It's like a bird picking a seed up off the path. If you don't let the truth in, a bird will take it away, and you will no longer have the opportunity for that truth to change your life. You heard the truth, but you didn't hear it." Don't be quick to push away challenging insights about purity.

---

24   Matthew 13:3-23, Mark 4:2-20, Luke 8:4-15

Another reason why the truth can't have its way in your life is that you resist it. The soil has to be soft enough to let the roots from a developing seed penetrate. Truth has a way of making life temporarily uncomfortable. Truth produces pressure. If your response to the demands truth can make on your life is to say "Ouch! If I'm going to believe that truth, then I'm going to have to change, and I don't know how I feel about that." You may well take truth on board only until you feel the pain of change and then begin to resist the truth again. Don't abort the work of truth on this journey.

One more reason why truth fails to do its work in you is that you don't give it the space, the time or the attention it deserves and the competing pressures of life choke it out. If you never think about it, don't nurture it, and don't give it any opportunity to bring insight to you, the truth won't help. That's one of the reasons I like to see men writing in their *Valiant Man Daily Journal* every day. It gives truth a chance. Some men can hear a lot of truth and yet never make progress. I've watched men take part in the Valiant Man program and turn up faithfully once a week with a bunch of other men, but between the weekly sessions they don't make time to revisit the truth. In a busy world it is easy to be so occupied with the pressures of life there's no space for truth to do its work in our lives. As a result, the truth gets choked.

But then Jesus said, "If you have a good, honest heart and you let the truth in, it will grow and produce change in your life." For some people, the change will be small—thirtyfold. For others there will be significant change—sixtyfold. Yet for others the change is like a miracle—a hundredfold. I've had men report to me, "Mate, I attended a Valiant Man program at my church and my entire life was turned upside down!" Well, that sounds like a hundredfold miracle to me!

The outcome of diligently following through with the content of this book will be different for every man, but every man who is teachable and who has a heart to let the truth in will harvest a crop of some kind. Some men will finish this book and say, "Some positive changes happened to me as I read that book. Thanks." Some men will be able to say, "My life was totally changed as I read the book—I've seen a hundredfold improvement." That's the power of truth. Jesus Christ, the greatest teacher the world has ever known, said, "If you will let truth in and if you will let your heart be open, you can change."

Deciding to let the truth in is a decision to step across that white line into the Arena of Healing—where a *good* man becomes a *valiant* man.

Attitude 4: Proactivity (the hungry)

Blessed are those who hunger and thirst for righteousness, for they will be filled.[25]

The power to succeed is conferred on those who hunger and thirst for righteousness. This is a call for you to be proactive, to embrace a godly goal and actively pursue it. Your goal is not instant gratification, it's being a decent man, a godly man, a *valiant man* – and the ones who are empowered to succeed are willing to take action to see it become reality.

The proactive (hungry) attitude says this:

I am determined to do whatever it takes to apply the truth I hear in the pursuit of necessary change. I am no longer willing to live with coping mechanisms as a way of life. My goal is to be an upright man. I want to be a valiant man, truly human and truly whole; I want to be right within my whole being.

25   Matthew 5:6

There is no guarantee of healing for those who are simply pursuing happiness or instant gratification. In fact when it comes to distortions in our sexuality that's what got us into trouble in the first place. We found out that we could get pleasant feelings through arousal of various kinds. We found sex was an avenue to pleasure that would work, and work every time. We found we could get immediate release and immediate mood change. Some of the distortions that have developed in our sexuality are the result of pursuing instant happiness and instant gratification. For those distortions to now be remedied, you and I are going to have to make uprightness a higher priority than instant happiness. If we aren't prepared to do that, if we aren't prepared to fight for uprightness over personal happiness, then we won't change.

We need to realize that being upright is firstly a gift that God gives. One of the most wonderful aspects about being a Christian is the knowledge that God sees you as a perfect man, a valiant man, from the moment you trust Jesus and set your heart to be like him. He gives this gift by faith. He will declare you to be a valiant man, if that is your desire; then having seen you as a *valiant man*, he wants you to walk into the reality of actually *being* the *valiant man* that he declares you to be. Righteousness is firstly a gift of God in Christ, and then it's a work of grace in the make-up of those who are willing to go beyond coping to develop character and to grow in uprightness. That truth has got to become real to you. God already thinks you are a *valiant man* if you have that goal in your heart. Then you need to walk that out and grow into that kind of a man in real life.

The choice you need to make is to be pro-active in the pursuit of consistent character. When you decide to accept responsibility to seek after the uprightness in your character that has been conferred on you by faith in Jesus, you walk across that white line—onto the field of blessing where you are empowered to fulfill the call on your life.

Are you ready to make choices, hard choices, and act on them? That's what this attitude is all about.

Attitude 5: Forgiveness (the merciful)

Blessed are the merciful,
for they will be shown mercy.[26]

If you want to become healthy, you are going to have to deal with issues of resentment and unforgiveness. You need to know you are forgiven yourself, and then adopt a forgiving attitude towards others. While Jesus said it first, the *Sexaholics Anonymous White-book* confirms this powerful insight. In the *Sexaholics Anonymous Whitebook* forgiveness is acknowledged as one of the key elements essential in the healing of sexual addiction and it will prove to be important in overcoming fractional addiction as well. *Sexaholics Anonymous* has observed that sexual behavior is often justified by feelings of hurt because he or she believes that somebody has done them wrong. The idea goes something like this: "I feel hurt and miserable so I deserve some sexual pleasure to compensate me for my pain". The person you perceive as having hurt you might be your wife, it might be God, or it might be someone else. In the search for sexual purity the power of forgiveness is not only vital in the undoing of shame and unworthiness, it has a role to play in resolving the very mechanisms that can fuel sexual addiction and give permission to acting out sexually inappropriate behavior.

Wounded people often rehearse their hurts. They let resent-

---

26   Matthew 5:7

ment recycle over and over again, rehearsing emotions like a wounded victim. *How terrible that the world has treated me like this,* they tell themselves. The more the mountain of injustice grows inside you, the more it justifies doing whatever it takes to feel better again. Of course, for a man sex is one of the greatest mood modifiers in his arsenal. He can approach sex as a mood-altering experience, knowing that when nothing else will work, sex will. Men who want to redevelop personal purity must pay attention to unresolved resentment because it is the resentment that gives them permission to act out sexually or to go somewhere else in their mind for a mood-altering experience. Sex is used as compensation for unresolved hurts.

The story of God's mercy and amazing grace toward you is the greatest story ever told. The reality of God's forgiveness through Jesus must be appreciated and accepted. To step over that white line and get into the Arena of Healing, you must embrace the mercy that is offered to you in Jesus, and you need to begin to exercise it in resolving the hurts you have accumulated in life. When you understand this attitude, it sounds something like this:

> *I acknowledge the centrality of amazing grace. I need forgiveness and I need help, neither of which I deserve. As I need forgiveness and help, I understand that others need it also. I will seek to help others experience what I am seeking for myself. I will open my heart to the needs of others as I desire to have others be open to me. I will forgive as I desire to be forgiven. I will cease judging as I desire to escape from judgment.*

One of the most important elements of your journey is going to be for you to grow in the certainty that God loves you. You cannot drive yourself to personal purity with whips of fear and shame. You can't beat yourself up, saying, "If I don't change, God won't like me."

There needs to be a sense that God loves you; that He has digni-fied you. You need to rise into what God has bestowed on you. It's called amazing grace; it's the love of God. The love of God is one of the greatest strengthening elements in a man's life.

The genius of this attitude is that as you release mercy to others, you become more aware of the fact that you yourself are a recipient of amazing grace. Jesus said, "Blessed are the merciful, for they will be shown mercy."[27] If you want the grace of God to work in your life, you are going to need to show grace. If you want to be able to live out a sense of being forgiven, you need to practice being a forgiver.

Resentful people can never feel like they've been forgiven. A man who will not forgive his wife, a man who will not release his wife from his personal expectations, says, "If only you gave me more sex, I wouldn't have to be so grumpy! If only you were more like the kind of woman I need, I would be okay!" That, my friend, is resentment. That is holding your wife in judgment. You must release her and allow her to simply be who she is. You need to ask God to give you grace to know how to nurture her, to lift her, and to see her not just as your provision but as a precious lamb that God gave you to treasure and die for first. If you can't find release from constantly judging her, you will never find the grace to grow into a *valiant man*. Being a *valiant man* involves sensing the pres-ence of God's grace and being free to forgive your wife and release her from the judgments you have formed about her supposed inad-equacies and supposed imperfections.

You and I need to embrace forgiveness. We need to learn to throw resentment out of our lives. Only those who are willing to forgive are able to fully live in the sense of being forgiven. None of us can afford the luxury of resentment and unforgiveness. To learn

---

27   Matthew 5:7

to totally and utterly forgive the weaknesses of others honors God and sets us free from the dangerous presence of resentment.

Step over that white line and into the Arena of Healing—choose mercy.

Attitude 6: Pure motives (the pure in heart)

Blessed are the pure in heart,
for they will see God.[28]

Motives are the secret reasons behind our actions. Growing from *good* man to *valiant* man is not just about learning new ways of behaving, and it certainly isn't about improving our appearance management skills. Growing from *good* man to *valiant* man is about addressing what is going on in the depths of your being. Out of your heart flow the issues of your life. What *really* motivates you to do what you do?

This attitude requires us to declare:

I will cease playing games and undertake a rigorous moral inventory
of my motives and behavior. I determine to discover every unhealthy
way within me and face it head on.

It is my hope that as you read this book you will begin to see some of the motives that bubble away inside you, causing you to feel certain feelings and desire certain actions. It is not enough to just change your behavior. You must reach into those hidden springs, those hidden desires and those hidden secret beliefs that make you who you are and produce the life you live.

One of the challenges you must face when it comes to understand-

28   Matthew 5:8

ing your motives is that your sexuality is often a very closely guarded secret. It may be so closely guarded that you don't really understand it yourself. You may never have permitted yourself to dwell on it and to really understand what is going on in the hidden springs and hidden desires of your heart. You can clothe it with such a level of secrecy that you don't even understand yourself, but unless you begin to get beyond that inability to know, you can't change.

Our inner belief system is a powerful thing. Patrick Carnes says that in every sex addict there lays the belief that he is not a valuable person in the eyes of others. A sex addict also believes that nobody would really want to meet his needs. A sex addict believes that if others knew what was truly going on inside him, they would reject him. Carnes says that whether he knows it or not, the person who has moved to sexual addiction has come to believe that sex is his greatest need.

A good friend shared with me how this insight helped him to break what had become a lifestyle of habitual masturbation. He despaired that the habit could ever be broken. He said to me, "When I read Patrick Carnes' book *Out of the Shadows*, I discovered the lie that had consumed my life. I had come to believe that sex was my greatest need. The moment I realized that lie was at the root of my habit, and that it *was* a lie, I knew I could beat that thing. And I did."

It may well be that as you read this book you will discover wrong motives and mis-beliefs lurking within your thought life that you have never suspected or identified. They may have remained hidden because you have never looked deep enough, or it may be because this part of your life has been kept a deliberate secret. I hope you will capture a fresh insight about what is motivating you, and when you do, my prayer is that you say to yourself, "Hey, I can beat that thing!" And you will!

Decide that you will examine your deepest motivations—and cross that white line on to the Arena of Healing.

Attitude 7: Healing love (the peacemaker)

Blessed are the peacemakers,
for they will be called sons of God.[29]

The *valiant man* needs to adopt the attitude that restoring peace to his most precious relationships is his highest priority. If you want the power to succeed, you are going to have to lift the healing of relationships above the meeting of your own personal needs.

In 1996 I attended a recovery conference in Boston, and in preparation for the creation of the Valiant Man program I took every class they had on sexual addiction. A number of the presenters said that when it comes to the issue of breaking severe sexual addiction, it is often necessary for periods of complete abstinence. They said that sexual addiction can grow to the point that a person no longer knows how to love or touch anybody without it being a sexual expression. If you are in that position, this attitude is vital: *I want to learn how to do healing love, not just sexual love. I want to learn how to heal my wife. I want to learn how we can truly care for one another.*

In dealing with entrenched sexual addiction, learning the difference between a truly loving sexual expression and a self indulgent sexual expression can require a significant season of sexual abstinence. Getting what we want sexually can become so wired into the behavior patterns of a man that he doesn't even know how to do healing love; he only knows how to do sexual expression. Thank-

---

29   Matthew 5:9

fully, most men will not require that degree of therapy to bring this attitude to bear in their marriage, but the concept remains the same. At its core, the meaning of life is the development of loving relationships and the *valiant man* has embraced the fact that it is more important for his wife to feel and know she is loved and treasured than it is for him to get his jollies.

My friend, if you want to be a valiant man and really connect with your wife, then you need to be able to express healing love. The attitude of healing love says this:

I am alive for relationship. I'm determined to be reconciled to God and reconciled to others. As much as I humanly can, I will seek to restore every broken relationship, especially the relationships in my own home.

We men have to face this critical issue of relationships. We are primarily alive for one reason, and that is to relate and to love. But men have a tendency to learn to do life in isolation. There are a couple of reasons for this. It's partly to do with a man's testosterone, and it's also partly to do with boys and their socialization.

Socially, boys tend to develop their personalities by pulling *away* from their mother, whereas girls tend to develop their personalities by doing things *with* their mother. Girls learn how to be girls by hanging around their mother, whereas boys have a tendency to climb trees, burn things down, and run off and do stuff that they don't want anybody to know about. They tend to develop their personalities in isolation from mum, and dad is rarely as accessible to take her place in those developmental years.

Add to that the impact of testosterone—the hormone of risk, daring and aggression. The natural competitiveness of males causes them to approach relationships differently. Boys have a tendency to grow up more independently and less relationally connected. But as we strive to become *valiant men*, we need to make a decision to work against that pattern. We have to learn to do relationships well. We have to learn to like people, to relate well to others, and to love them, and that includes God.

I was present in a men's conference where a highly loved and respected pastor and author was transparent enough to describe the development of masturbation in his life as "a lonely act of self indulgence". You and I are not alive for lonely acts of self indulgence, we are alive for relationships. We are going to work on this aspect of our lives like we have never worked on it before.

Step across that white line, you *valiant man*! Make a decision to devote yourself to the healing of your relationships as *your* highest priority.

Attitude 8: Courage (the persecuted)

Blessed are those who are persecuted because of righteousness, for theirs is the kingdom of heaven.[30]

As you set out to become a *valiant man*, you are going to find yourself between a rock and a hard place. Your old sexual habits and desires will try to drag you in an unhelpful direction. When you resist those habits and desires and attempt to go in the right direction, you will feel a level of pain and tension. It's like being persecuted. As you seek to move forward your old brain wiring will fight with you and resist change. There may be demonic elements that want to resist your progress. You may even find that old friends and people from past relationships will want to drag you back to where you came from. If you want to be a *valiant man* it's going to take courage.

---

30   Matthew 5:10

The attitude of courage sounds like this:
*I am determined to pursue what is right and to pursue wholeness,
no matter what the cost. With or without the approval of others
I am determined to press forward and do the right thing. I determine to be undeterred by emotional pressures, spiritual pressures
or the pressure of others who would prefer me to remain as I am.*

The question I put to you is this: Do you still want to be a *valiant man*? If you do, then here is the challenge: pay the price; put up or shut up! If you are willing to begin the journey from *good* man to *valiant man*, pull on your armor, draw your sword, and suck up the pain.

At this stage, it is important for you to know that God is OK with you encountering some suffering on the journey. In fact, the Bible says, "We also rejoice in our sufferings, because we know that suffering produces perseverance; perseverance, character; and character, hope."[31] And the Book of James says, "Consider it pure joy, my brothers, whenever you face trials of many kinds, because you know that the testing of your faith develops perseverance."[32] In other words, consider it pure joy when the pressure comes on, because it is in those moments that the best work that God has to do in your life will ever be done. If you don't understand that, you will become confused and make wrong choices when you get part way down this experience of becoming a *valiant man* and the old pressures and temptations will start to pull you back to the old lifestyle.

Maybe it's an old passion for pornography you're up against. Maybe it's an old desire to get back on that phone and do phone sex. Maybe it's a longing to log on to a website and download some erotic nonsense. Maybe it's an urge to go rent an R-rated DVD.

31   Romans 5:3-4
32   James 1:2-3

Maybe it's that old pattern of life drawing you back to purchase a pornographic magazine. Maybe it's a deadly urge to risk a visit to a prostitute. There will be some huge pressures from the past that you will face from time to time. Jesus won't mind that you are facing tough and painful pressures at all. He felt it in the Garden of Gethsemane. He had to go through the battle himself. He had to show courage in the fight to get the right thing done. Now it's your turn. Stand up and face the pressure, you *valiant man*.

Let me tell you why God doesn't mind you facing those pressures. It is because it's your experience of pushing through that produces the character and the change you are longing for. A valiant man can only ever become a valiant man by taking a stand when the heat is on and the wind is in his face. You become the man you long to be as you take another step into the pain rather than running away from it.

Yes, sir! It will take courage. One last thing: don't try and go it alone. I encourage you to stand together with other men as you face these battles. When those tough moments come, have some friends' phone numbers handy. You may never have done this before. It may be difficult for you to do this. It will take an act of humility and courage for you to phone a guy one night and say, "Hey, listen. I'm struggling." However, it will be in those moments where you exercise humility and courage that you will begin to break through.

REFLECTION

To become a *valiant man* you will need to adopt these eight attitudes. The reason I have placed these eight attitudes at the beginning of the book is that they are the key to all healing and all restoration.

The value of the rest of this book is determined by your willingness to embrace these attitudes. If you learn to adopt them by the time you finish this book, you will make significant progress towards a *valiant manhood* that will contribute powerfully to your family, your church, your community and to your God.

Get out of the grandstand, mate.

Embrace the attitudes.

Cross the white line, enter the Arena of Healing and get in the game.

The *blessing* awaits you.

CHAPTER 3

THE SEXUAL MAN

"Man is the only animal that blushes. Or needs to."
Mark Twain

"Men live in a fantasy world. I know this because I am one,
and I actually receive my mail there."
Scott Adams

For years I have punished myself for having sexual desires, especially if I felt those desires toward someone other than my wife. I was taught that when you are married you lose all sexual feelings toward other women. I now realize how stupid this is. I have never been unfaithful to my wife, whom I love dearly, but I just don't seem to be able to stop my sexual feelings from running amuck.

I don't want these feelings; they are driving me crazy. But I don't seem to be able to get rid of them. The harder I try, the stronger they become. What is it with this sexual stuff? The more you try to forget or ignore it, the more it drives you crazy.[33]

This could be the honest, heartfelt cry of *any* man living on this planet today. Whilst it's actually an experience described in Dr. Archibald Hart's book *The Sexual Man*, the fact is that it describes the battle every man faces almost daily.

It is vitally important for men to understand their maleness. It is complex, confusing and chaotic. In Chapter One I described the multi-faceted call of manhood. To become a *valiant man*, you must see yourself as having the face of an ox, the face of a lion, the face of an eagle, and the face of a man. These four faces represent the multi-faceted challenges you confront each day as a man.

The face of an ox represents the call to be a man who works hard, who serves, who labors, and who provides. Why does a man go to work all the days of his life and bring home his pay to provide for his wife and family? Because it is one of the jobs he has been given—to be an ox. The face of a lion speaks of the man as guardian; a leader of his own home, a leader in his church, a leader in his community, and a protector of the weak. The face of an eagle

---

33   A Hart, *The Sexual Man*, Word Publishing, 1994, pp 3-4.

speaks of us as a man of God, a man of prayer, a man of worship, and a man who knows how to touch heaven.

Into this mix we must insert the fourth face—that of a man. The *valiant man* is a man with hormones, a man with a physical body that makes demands and creates pressures that he has to deal with constantly. You can hear men across the globe crying out, "How do I get rid of this stuff? How do I handle this pressure? It's driving me crazy!" That, my friend, is the face of a man. It's the earthy, hormonal, horny side of the sexual man. The fact is that every one of us has to deal with this dimension of ourselves, for we are all sexual men. We must learn to manage our humanity well.

In the same book I quoted at the beginning of this chapter, Dr. Archibald Hart says:

> Why doesn't religion remove these sexual feelings? It is because religious men have the same physical bodies as everyone else. From the moment the sex hormones start to flow, the male begins a battle. It is a battle for control, and the male who doesn't engage in this battle is dangerous to women and society. Many rapists, for instance, are men who have given up struggling to control their sex drive. Sadists and even sexual serial killers have done the same. But what about ordinary boys and men? For almost every male of every age, the sex drive is a powerful and urgent feeling, demanding his immediate attention.[34]

In the words of the famous physicist Julius Sumner Miller, "Why is it so?" We have got to ask the same question: Why are we men like that? It helps to know what's behind all this pressure. Not that understanding it makes it go away, but in knowing you begin to understand how normal you really are.

---

34   ibid. p 6.

Part of your journey from good man to valiant man is confronting the feelings of defectiveness and shame so commonly associated with male sexuality. You are a man with a physical body, and when you understand the make-up of a man it begins to make sense as to why this pressure is so relentless and why it has to be every man's battle. Rather than beating yourself up over that, let's just get on with the job and realize how normal the struggle really is.

The making of a male

Now, here's a bit of science for you to digest. The human body is constructed from the information that is encoded along 46 ribbons of information—46 strands of DNA called chromosomes—clustered in 23 pairs. Those 23 pairs of chromosomes carry all the information needed to build a human being. The sex cells—the sperm and the ovum—are the only cells in the body that don't have 46 chromosomes. The sperm and the ovum contain only 23 chromosomes, a random sample of 50 percent of the father or the mother's DNA.

A new human being is the result of bringing the sperm cell with its 23 chromosomes together with the ovum and its 23 chromosomes. In conception, when a sperm and ovum unite, the 23 chromosomes from the sperm join the party with the 23 from the ovum. At that point, you've got the full complement; you've got all the information to make a new and unique human being!

The chromosome that carries the information for building a female is called the X chromosome, and the chromosome that carries the information for building a male is called the Y chromosome. A female carries a pair of X chromosomes in her genetic pool while a male carries one X and one Y chromosome in his genetic pool. And it's that one little chromosome, that one tiny Y chromosome out of 46, which separates the genders.

Since the only genetic information for gender a woman carries in her cells are two X chromosomes, when it comes to her sex cells—the ovum—every single one of them carries the X chromosome. When it comes to dividing up her DNA to pack half the information in a sex cell, all a woman brings to the equation is the information for another female. Every ovum in a woman's body is voting for another female. They're ganging up on us, guys.

When it comes to the sperm cell, us guys are much more democratic. Since our DNA carries both an X and a Y chromosome, the sperm cells end up with a 50/50 split—half the sperm cells carry an X chromosome and half the sperm cells carry a Y chromosome. How fair can you get? A man's sperm votes half the time for a new male and half the time for a new female. I personally feel really good about that.

If a sperm carrying the X chromosome wins the race to find an ovum, it joins with the X chromosome in the ovum and you get two X chromosomes, which means that a female has been conceived. If a sperm with a Y chromosome wins the race, then you get an X chromosome and a Y chromosome, which means that a male has been conceived.

The miracle involved in the making of a male is stunning. Your mother was born with more than a lifetime's supply of eggs or ova. Alternating between the right and left ovaries, one was released each month throughout her childbearing years. Your father had testes capable of producing an average of 300 million sperm every day in his peak fertility years. How come it takes 300 million sperm to fertilize just one egg? Because, being the male contribution, they just won't stop and ask directions—so it takes that many for just one of them to luck out and find their way!

Once a sperm has won the race and pierced the ovum, an invisible shield forms to prevent another sperm from entering. When you think of all the different combinations of genetic material that are possible in both the sperm and the ovum, and when you think of how unique the ultimate combination of sperm and ovum actually is, you need to acknowledge that you are the winner of a lottery of unimaginable proportions. Once a sperm pierces the ovum, the fertilized egg plants itself in the wall of the uterus, and this is where the baby will develop.

Stage 1: Forming the male genitals

From a very early stage the embryo is clearly a human being, but if the baby was lost before the tenth week, you would assume that the child had been a girl. Initially, the external genitals and the internal reproductive system develop along a female model.

When God created sex in the first place, He built a male model first (called Adam). He then took a portion of that man and differentiated that portion into the female version (called Eve). In the womb that process works in reverse. In the making of a male child the process starts with a basic female pattern and differentiates it back to the male through its development in the womb.

In the first ten weeks of a baby's development, the mother's X chromosome dominates its appearance. Every male bears the marks of his mother on his chest. Those two nipples on your chest are the marks of the X chromosome, a reminder for life of your debt to your mum. If a Y chromosome is present in the fetus, it will begin to make its demands around the sixth week. That Y chromosome triggers a release of androgens (or male hormones) and they begin the transformation of the genital organs from female to male.

Every man commences life with two little gonads inside his body, a little fallopian tube, and all the female machinery—outside and inside. In about the ninth week there is a chemical transformation that breaks the ovaries loose and brings them down the fallopian tube like a highway and allows those little gonads to move down and outward towards the place where the scrotum will eventually be. At this stage there is an open vagina there, not a scrotum. The clitoral pleasure centre begins to enlarge to form the penis. The vaginal lips begin to enlarge to form a scrotum to hold the gonads thus forming the testes. The vagina then seals shut and leaves a bright red, raised scar that is visible from the base of the scrotum around the front and up the entire lower side of the penile shaft. You will find that line there for the rest of your life. It is part of the amazing transformation process in forming the sexual man.

The first part of this process, called by some the 'Splitting of the Adam', is accomplished by a miracle of chemistry. The chemistry involved dissolves the fallopian tubes and preserves the tiny undeveloped uterus where it hangs from the urinary tract of the boy for the rest of his life. That is stage one in the development of the sexual man. It is the stage that sets the genitals in the right place and in the right shape.

Stage 2: The wiring of the male brain

The genitals are not the only parts that begin with a feminine pattern. The standard model brain is female. Connected by a bundle of fibers called the corpus callosum, the female brain is organized with open communication between the left hemisphere and the right hemisphere. Every brain contains millions of androgen sensitive cells and fibers. They are designed to dissolve and disappear on contact with male hormones. The Y chromosome triggers a flood of androgens from the mother and the baby boy's testes when the little testicles arrive.

From around the 16th to the 26th week a baby boy's head is swimming with male chemicals. The androgen sensitive cells and fibers dissolve and disappear. The corpus callosum loses about 25 million fibers, and what remains is the male brain modified for specialized tasks. A significant transformation of the brain has taken place.

If you would like more information on this subject, try Donald Joy's book *Bonding: Relationships in the Image of God* and another book called *Brain Sex*. Both books are mentioned in the Bibliography.

There is always a danger when talking in generalities about men and women. Stereotypes are rarely helpful. However, the rewiring of the male brain produces population distinctives between the male population and the female population that in some cases are significant and in other cases absolute. For example, when it comes to sensitivity to touch, the least sensitive woman is still more sensitive than the most sensitive man. That's an absolute distinctive. Without getting into a subject much broader than the scope of this book, suffice it to say that the re-wiring of the male brain results in significant distinctives between male and female populations and their sexual responses.

The primary hormone involved in brain rewiring is testosterone. Its presence or absence seems to be the most powerful organizer of the way our brains function. Males are born not only with a penis and testicles; they are born with a brain that was formed by the action of testosterone. If you are a male, there were adjustments made to your brain in your early development, and the wiring of your brain was done by testosterone. From the earliest weeks you can see the action of this differentiated brain in the way baby girls relate and the way baby boys relate. When you give little girls in kindergarten some boys' toys to play with, like toy trucks, you will frequently find the trucks will talk to each other! But when you give boys the same toys, you'll see the trucks bashing each other and making noises like *bang, boom, crash* and *brrrrrrrrr!* Being a boy is significantly a matter of the way their brain is wired.

Stage 3: Adolescence and the brain's response to erotic images

The third stage of a man's sexual development sees childhood give way to adolescence. This is the stage when the body runs a check over all of its systems and gives the go-ahead for puberty to occur over a two-year period. First, a growth spurt can add an inch a month in height. The voice also begins to deepen. Testosterone triggers muscular development that takes the body from about 23% muscle—the standard experience of a child and a woman—and transforms the body into something like 40% muscle when a man is at his best physical development. Shoulders widen and hair appears on the face, groin, chest, arms, legs and arm pits. Body chemistry begins to produce the male pheromone with its pungent odors. The penis and testicles increase in size. Sperm and seminal fluid production begins; the pressure of sperm and seminal production triggers frequent spontaneous erections and occasional spontaneous ejaculation.

The gift of a huge pleasure potential has been bestowed on the man, and the need to discipline that sexual gift is vital for many reasons. These developments that take place during puberty take the original wiring—the original sexual equipment—and move it into that third stage, in which the sexual man begins to function.

Now, there are characteristics of exposure to prenatal testosterone. The male that has formed along normal male development patterns is the way he is, at least in part, because he has a Y chromosome and because of the action of testosterone, both in his body and on his brain. Testosterone has accomplished specialization and organization of the typical male brain. But testosterone has also *energized* that male brain. Testosterone is the hormone of risk, daring and aggression. This is one of the reasons why the largest demographic in prisons is young men between the ages of 18 and 28. It manifests itself in the way young men drive their first car and that propensity for risk, daring and aggression can all too easily end in a tragedy of twisted metal and dead young people.

The big question is this: Can we keep these young men alive long enough for sanity to catch up with this hormonal drive that tends to make them aggressive and daring, often to the point of suicide or self-destruction? That's why energetic, rough-and-tumble play and aggression are hallmarks of the organization of the male brain. It is the young male with his body busting with testosterone that will pick a fight, who will break and enter homes, and who will press his desire for sex to the point of rape. While you cannot excuse that behavior by saying, "Hormones made me do it!" It is a reality of life we must take into account. Young men have all the daring, boldness, drive and energy in the world, and yet, all too often, insufficient brains or experience to go along with it!

One of the greatest needs for young men during this period of time is the guiding hand of a good man who has done the trip before him; an older, wiser man who is prepared to help the younger man successfully make it through this period. Young men need a lot of help because they are under a great degree of pressure.

Men are stirred by erotic images

As already stated, the male brain, rewired by testosterone, demonstrates population distinctives when compared with the female brain. Try and name a single world renowned female composer. Women can play instruments, so why is there not one female composer to stand alongside Brahms, Beethoven, Liszt, Chopin, Rachmaninov, Handel or Schubert? It's a brain wiring issue. Men have a population advantage in that area of brain function.

A similar distinctive emerges when comparing the management of things versus people. Within days of birth, a female child will watch a real human face for twice as long as a geometric object hung over the crib. A male child will watch the human face and the geometric object with about equal interest. Interest in relationships is not just about socialization; it's also a brain wiring issue. Women as a population have an advantage when it comes to relationships in terms of brain wiring. Men can do relationships too, but they find as life unfolds that *things* are easier to manage than *people*, and thus they drift towards the garden shed.

However, it is in the area of sexual arousal that one of these brain distinctives emerges with significant implications for life. The male brain has been rewired by hormonal action in the womb. The hormone of greatest influence in that process is testosterone. Testosterone is not only the hormone of muscular development, risk, daring and aggression. It is the hormone of libido – of sexual desire. Remove testosterone from the human system and sexual desire evaporates. Thus, if a female walks naked into the presence of a male, the impact on the male is instantaneous and profound. If a male walks naked into the presence of a female, she is likely to simply burst out laughing. One of the traits of the wiring of your male brain is the connection between your eyeballs and the sexual arousal chemistry set in your brain. You will be profoundly impacted, stirred and aroused by erotic images.

It is important for you to know that this is not the result of some *deficiency* in a man's moral fibre; it is a *feature* of the wiring of your brain. You have got to understand and appreciate the significance of this aspect of being a male. It is the normal trait of a brain that is formed by testosterone and fuelled by testosterone.

The word *pornography* is derived from the ancient Greek word *pornea*, which in early days carried the meaning "the writings of the prostitutes". Prostitutes have always known that men are highly responsive to erotic images. In ancient civilizations prostitutes would draw pictures of breasts and of sexual intercourse on the walls near their dwellings, so when men walked past they would be aroused by their sexual depictions. That's how the prostitutes would generate new business; they would stir up the guys by putting up erotic images on the walls.

The male brain is susceptible to those images, whereas a woman could walk past and say, "Who did that? That's ridiculous! That's a bad drawing!", and walk on unaffected by those images. Now, I want to make a very important statement here. This is where men are prone to make a really vital mistake. Men *know* they are stirred by erotic images. It might be a sex scene in a movie. It might be a nude picture hanging on a wall in the workshop. It might be the sight of a woman taking her clothing off. It doesn't matter what it is, men **like** the feelings that seeing can produce. They tell themselves, *I can handle it. I can keep it under control.* Wrong! We can't handle it at all.

My friend, males are not wired to handle those experiences. I don't mean that one look and our behavior is out of control. On the outside you may well look totally under control. What I mean is that sexual arousal is not voluntary. The chemistry set in your head devoted to sexual arousal is triggered just by looking. All you have to do is *see* an erotic image, and that chemistry set starts the arousal process. When you are confronted by an erotic image, you have got to stop saying to yourself, *I think I can handle this. I can cope with a small amount of this. I can let some of it in and I'll know when to say, 'That's enough!'* You must understand that as a man you can't handle it. You are not wired up to handle it. If you can admit that to yourself, if you can accept that reality, it can be the beginning of a transforming experience in your life.

On the other hand, you could continue saying to yourself, *Ah, no, no! You don't understand. I **can** handle it!* So you give yourself permission to keep on looking and the outcome is sexual arousal because your wiring makes your eyeballs a gateway to the chemistry set inside your own head. The male brain, formed by the action of testosterone, is triggered by erotic images and you can't stop it. You can't manipulate that chemistry set in your head. If the images get in, the chemicals begin to mix and the process is underway. You simply can't handle that.

Highs through the eyes

This experience could be accurately described as 'highs through the eyes'. Men get their kicks through the eyes first. It's a fact that a man can get a high just by looking at a woman. She doesn't have to be provocatively dressed; she just needs to be attractive. The eyes see, the brain begins mixing those chemicals, and the high begins. It happens so easily it can sneak up on you and take the steering wheel before you are aware of what you are doing. You may be simply leafing through magazines and a picture triggers a little hit. Before you realize it you're looking for another, searching for the high that you get when you see pictures that have some measure of erotic content because you like the hit that it gives you. You might sit there flicking through the television channels at night; to the outside observer there's no cause for concern, but inwardly there's a vague hope that you might stumble across something that will set off that high. We are vulnerable to that mood-altering encounter of sexual arousal.

Men can get highs through their eyes. The chemistry of arousal is so powerful that men can easily learn that 'highs through the eyes' are the best thrills a man can get. If you want to train an animal to perform in a certain way you give little rewards every time an action is repeated. Men are trained for impurity in the same way. These constant little "rewards" train men to live this way, constantly tuned into jolts of sexual arousal in almost every circumstance of life, reacting to every opportunity for that high. A man may be driving in his car when suddenly a female jogger runs past and his mind registers; *Whoa! Yeah, got one again!* He sees a billboard on the freeway and again the instant reaction is; *Whoa! I saw it again!* A young lady may be crossing the road and instantly his brain reacts; *Oh, beautiful! I saw it again.*

It can happen moment by moment throughout the very normal experiences of the day. If your eyes are allowed to look and the chemistry begins bubbling, you can experience one little thrill after another all day long. This tendency to be feeding emotionally on little hits of sexual arousal through the eyes, moment by moment throughout the day can so easily become a man's way of life, and there is a very useful term to describe it; *junk sex.*

Just imagine for a moment that you decided to go and eat something at McDonald's every 30 minutes from dawn to dusk. Twenty times during the day you nibbled away on those burgers and chips—*nibble, nibble, nibble.* By the end of the day, your appetite would be shot to pieces. You could go home and sit down at the table to the best meal your wife could cook, and yet you would sit there turned off, unable to get excited about this delicious dinner—and it would have nothing to do with her cooking. The problem would be your jaded appetite. You nibbled so often and for so long that now nothing seems attractive to you.

That's what junk sex does for your relationship with your wife.

If you've been nibbling on these experiences all day long, it wouldn't matter how beautiful your wife is. If you have been drawing your sexual energy from one woman after another, one scene after another, one circumstance after another, it wouldn't matter who your wife is. After constant junk sex, you would find yourself jaded and somehow vaguely disinterested in your wife at home—no matter how wonderful she is.

It has always fascinated me that some of the most attractive women in the world don't keep their husbands. Why does that happen? Why would it be that film star Elizabeth Taylor had eight husbands? Why would Tom Cruise get bored with Nicole Kidman? You see, if a guy is doing junk sex, it wouldn't matter how attractive his wife is, he would find himself losing interest in her if he had fed himself with junk sex all day.

A man's eyes give him the opportunity to feed on junk sex. He feeds a sexual appetite without reference to his own wife and so the quality of the relationship with his wife degenerates. The relationship erodes because he's doing something that damages his appetite for his own wife, yet he may not even be aware of what he is doing.

Proverbs 27:7 says, "He who is full loathes honey, but to the hungry even what is bitter tastes sweet." When you ruin your sexual appetite through junk sex you end up loathing the honey that's in your own home. If you are ruining your appetite for the honey at home by investing your sexuality in pornography the impact is even more severe. If you have a wife she deserves better, and so do you.

Set boundaries for yourself

So what boundaries do we need to set? Let's look at three passages in the Bible. In Job 31:1, Job said this: "I made a covenant with my eyes not to look lustfully at a girl." That's a standard boundary—to make a covenant with your eyes. To make a covenant you would need to declare to yourself, *I will no longer allow my eyes to be used as a gateway to the chemistry set of arousal in my own head.*

The words of Jesus powerfully confirm the importance of this boundary. This is what Jesus said:

"You have heard that it was said, 'Do not commit adultery.' But I tell you that anyone who looks at a woman lustfully has already committed adultery with her in his heart. If your right eye causes you to sin, gouge it out and throw it away. It is better for you to lose one part of your body than for your whole body to be thrown into hell."[35]

You have got to realize that for a man the danger starts with the eyes. So you need to do whatever it takes to get your eyes under control, because it can take a man to hell. That's how I lost four good friends in a single year, four friends who were knocked out of well-known ministries. They were making a significant difference in people's lives, but they did not have this area under control. Jesus is saying, "You have got to realize there's a lot at stake here, and the eyes play a critical role in the problem. Don't look at a woman lustfully. If you look at a woman lustfully, your chemistry set will kick in and you're already on the road of moral impurity." Jesus is saying, "You have got to do whatever it takes to get this under control."

Here's another statement Jesus made:

"The eye is the lamp of the body. If your eyes are good, your whole body will be full of light. But if your eyes are bad, your whole body will be full of darkness. If then the light within you is darkness, how great is that darkness!"[36]

---

35   Matthew 5:27-29
36   Matthew 6:22-23

In other words, Jesus said, "What you are looking at, and what you allow yourself to dwell on, will determine whether you are full of light or darkness." The battle for your eyes is the first place you are going to need to win if you are going to become a valiant man, and if you are going to recover the kind of moral and spiritual health that you need.

If only we could teach teenage young men from their earliest days to understand the impact of looking and so to guard their eyes, we could raise young men with unique spiritual qualities. If they were helped and discipled to guard their eyes and to keep themselves from the more serious infections that take place once pornography becomes a part of a man's diet, we would raise young men who possess a healthy sense of self confidence. If a man is weak in this area, it erodes his sense of dignity and self confidence. It causes him to not like himself very much. If a man can maintain the purity of his eyes, then his moral and spiritual immune system will not easily be overcome.

We know that AIDS invades the body and destroys the immune system; then even the mildest of infections can take a man out. If a man has AIDS, he has no capacity to fight back against infections. If pornography has been part of your diet, then you have got to recognize that your immune system will have been damaged and it is going to require stricter protocols for you to be able to get well again and recover your sense of dignity. Don't take this next paragraph lightly; it is your escape route to a healthy life.

Bounce your eyes

Here is what you need to do: Learn to bounce your eyes. If you find yourself walking into an office and you suddenly become aware of a woman's beauty, look away; turn or bounce your eyes away. If you are driving down the road and you see a female jogger run past, when you start to turn your head, stop and say to yourself; *That's not my business!* And look elsewhere. When you are driving along the road and you see a billboard with a woman featured prominently, you'll start to look up, but stop... and bounce your eyes away. Every time you make the deliberate choice to bounce your eyes away, you are confirming a moral decision. You are building a character. You are behaving like a *valiant man*. Even a *good* man will want to look, but a *valiant* man will learn to control his eyes.

I know the power of this behavior because I've made it my own practice. I learned the principle from Arterburn and Stoeker who teach it in their book *Every Man's Battle*. I made a decision that before I tried to teach other men to avert their eyes I needed to prove its value myself. At first I was surprised at how often I had to do it. I began to think to myself; *where can a man look?* In highly sexualized western societies, you can't even safely read a newspaper or watch a television program—including the news—without realizing that at any moment you may need to avert your eyes. Over and over I found myself turning my eyes away. Over and over I found myself exclaiming; *Whoa, that's not my business!* And I bounced my eyes away.

Initially I was stunned at how frequently I had to do this. Then over the next few weeks I found myself aware of a rising delight in—and appreciation for—my own wife, and a rising sense of personal dignity. You see, these were the rewards that came with the battle. And yes, it was challenging. It took me about six weeks to win that war. If you bounce your eyes for six weeks, you *will* win this war. I continue the practice to this day.

Because we are attracted to sexual images, men tend to bounce their eyes *towards* them. That's why advertising is filled with sexual images. Advertisers know that placing a woman's body in an advertisement will make men look. Putting sexually attractive images in advertisements will cause men to turn and look. The male brain formed by testosterone is aroused through the eyeball.

My friend, it requires a moral decision to refuse to allow your life to be manipulated by everything that you can possibly look at. This is the beginning of the battle. It has to start with your control over your eyes. Like pulling your hand away from a hot stove, you must develop a reflex to bounce your eyes away. As you reach out and start to feel the heat, pull your hand right back. Train your mind to react immediately by saying, *Whoa, that's hot. I don't want to touch that!*

I literally learned to do that when I was a child. I burned my leg on a wood stove when I was about nine or ten years of age. The searing pain of my leg up against the glass of that wood stove was shocking. I never wanted to go near that stove again. Well, you and I need to develop a sense of that same searing danger when it comes to our eyes. You and I have got to *immediately* remove our eyes from an image, a person or a circumstance that we know has that sexualized aspect to it. Our reaction to turn away must be immediate.

By now you're probably asking questions like, what is lust, and how long do I have to look before it's classified as lust? Well, the answer is simply this: Long enough to create a chemical high. Long enough for you to realize that *Whoa, this is an erotic moment!* And long enough for you to know that your gaze has a certain feeling attached to it. If you maintain your look that long, then it has become lust.

Understand your weaknesses

You and I become aware of the situations in which we are most vulnerable. What circumstances present you with your Achilles heel? I know mine and you need to know yours. Because I regularly use the internet for my work, I am grateful the internet is not an issue for me. I have no desire, no temptation whatsoever, to look at pornography on the internet. That's not my weakness. But I do know this, that if I am watching a movie and a sex scene begins to unfold, that for me is dynamite. We all have a tendency to give ourselves approval for certain things we do that may be considered wrong. This is one of the ways we do it: "Oh, it's in context, you know. I'm watching that program in context." My friend, you weren't designed for that context. You weren't manufactured to be able to cope with that. As sophisticated, 21st century, media savvy individuals, we love to think we can handle it all, but we can't.

So you have to understand where your weakness is. It could be television programs with sexual encounters. Or it could be beachwear. For example, you could find yourself having great difficulty going to the beach because you keep looking everywhere. If that's you, then you need to say, *I can't be here at this stage in my life. This is not something I'm designed for.*

We men are bombarded with it… lingerie advertisements, female joggers, movies with sex scenes, a woman at work wearing a low-cut blouse, magazines featuring sexy women, soft porn internet images, and hard porn magazines. Be honest about where you are most vulnerable. We so easily justify skirting around the edges. It lowers the guilt threshold in our conscience. It starts as a little crack in the door: "Oh, I can handle it!" But it opens the door gradually, and in comes the danger.

A male has many ways of indulging in junk sex without ever seeing himself as indulging in sexual sin. Indulging destroys your appetite and does to your soul what eating junk food many times a day does to your body. You have got to develop an effective way of handling each challenge. When Jesus said, "If your right eye causes you to sin, gouge it out and throw it away!"[37] What he was saying was this: "Do not draw lines and say, 'Well, that's a bit extreme isn't it? I mean, I wouldn't take that step because that would be over the top.'" When it comes to guarding your eternal destiny, there is nothing that is over-the-top... nothing!

REFLECTION

The standards for purity that your community may have set are very well intentioned. But you and I must adopt our own higher standards for purity. If it requires that you disconnect your house from the internet, then you need to do that quickly. If it means that you should stop going to the movies, then don't go to the movies. If it means you can't watch television, then get rid of the television set. The fact is, it isn't good enough to say, "Well, other people can manage it, so why can't I!" That's not the issue. The question is, can *you* manage it? Are you winning this battle? Because if you're not winning the battle, Jesus says you've got to be prepared to do whatever it takes to win the battle... whatever it takes! So make up your mind—are you ready to win?

---

37   Matthew 5:29

Chapter 4

The Origin, Power & Purpose of Sex

"It is with our passions, as it is with fire and water, they are good servants but bad masters."
Aesop

"You have to accept the fact that part of the sizzle of sex comes from the danger of sex. You can be overpowered."
Camille Paglia

Clear goals are very valuable things. They help you set your direction and keep you focused on the big issues. Goals help you to be honest with where you are now and with where you want to go. When it comes to the management of this powerful gift in your life—your sexuality—it helps to see the goal clearly.

I believe the Apostle Paul summed it up really well in the Bible:

> For this is the will of God, your sanctification: that you abstain from sexual immorality; that each one of you knows how to control his own body in holiness and honor, not in the passion of lust like the Gentiles who do not know God.[38]

My friend, that's your goal. God wants you to set your life apart. He wants you to be able to keep yourself from sexual immorality. He wants you to know how to control your body, to have your body held in holiness and in honor, and to make sure you are not driven by lust, which is so common in our world today.

Men face sexual challenges and some of them will never, ever go away. I have said before that ministers of religion don't fail because they forget they're Christians, they fail because they forget they're human. The fact is that some of that humanity will never go away. Forget trying to pray it away. Forget praying to be so spiritual that temptations never impact you. Sexual challenges are a part of your humanity.

Whilst we know those challenges will never go away, we *can* begin to focus on what we *are able* to change. One of the reasons men are reading this book and taking part in Valiant Man programs is that they know their sexuality presents a challenge and they are keen to learn how to handle that challenge appropriately and honorably.

To manage this powerful area of your life well, we need a good

---

38   1 Thessalonians 4:3-5, ESV

theology of sex. Man cannot live by rules alone. It wouldn't be possible to create a rule that would keep you safe in every circumstance. Eventually you are going to have to learn to live out of the purpose for which sex was created. So we need to deal with questions like, where did sex come from? How did it ever come to exist? And why does sex possess so much power for good and for harm?

Your sexuality comes from God

I am a rampant creationist. I do not believe the origin of sex is to be found in evolutionary accidents. If our origin could be traced back to pre-existent matter, atoms and molecules, chemistry and physics, then our sexuality would be nothing more than physical. If that was the case it would be possible to understand our sexual passions by reference to the physical world alone. However, the fact is that you are not an animal. We are not the end product of a mindless machine.

The Bible says:

In the beginning was the Word, and the Word was with God, and the Word was God. He was with God in the beginning. Through him all things were made; without him nothing was made that has been made.[39]

Our sexuality comes from the hand of God, so if we are going to understand our sexuality, then we are going to have to understand something about the nature of God, particularly because God said, "Let us make man in our image, in our likeness… So God created man in his own image, in the image of God he created him; male and female he created them."[40]

Sex reveals something about God's divine nature. You will

39   John 1:1-3
40   Genesis 1:26, 27

never understand yourself and you won't understand your sexuality without understanding something about the nature of God. An issue of profound importance is this: the Bible teaches that God is a trinity; it is one of the unique elements of Christianity. Christianity teaches that the God who created the heavens and the earth is not a lonely singularity; he is a trinity of distinguishable persons, yet so intimate in relationship as to share indivisible substance. That's a mouthful that deserves to be unpacked.

Imagine for a moment that the Unitarians are right, that God is not a trinity, but a singularity; imagine that God is a single person in a single substance. If that was true, consider the implications. God is the only uncreated reality. God is the only being that never had a beginning. Everything that exists has been created by God. If God is a person who exists from all eternity in absolute aloneness, absolute singularity, and everything that exists owes its origin to God, where would love ever come from? How would sex ever come to exist? Where would the idea of intimacy ever come from? Where would the idea of communion and relationship ever come from? If God creates out of his own being, like an artist paints out of his personality, how would love, intimacy, relationship, communication, communion, all the greatest things in life, ever come to exist?

God loves intimacy

The Bible does not reveal a creator who is a lonely singularity, inhabiting eternity in solitary confinement. The Bible speaks of God as a trinity of persons, and the word that makes the trinity accessible is the word *intimacy*. For centuries theologians struggled to describe how three distinguishable persons could be one. The theological term they developed to try to make sense of what the Bible reveals about this aspect of God was the word *perichoresis*, which means "being-in-one-another", "permeation without confusion", and "having room for one another".

The trinity is one of the most important revelations in the Bible. The three persons of the Godhead are distinguishable—they are real persons. The human comparison in my marriage is this: I am a person, and my wife is a person; you can distinguish between the two of us. The Godhead is three persons, yet they exist in such everlasting intimacy as to share an indivisible substance. In substance they are one.

Perichoresis is a term to describe a relationship so intimate that it means, *I am in you and you are in me, and yet you are real and I am real - you are a person and I am a person. We are so intimate as to share the same substance without one person ever submerging or overwhelming the distinguishable personality of the other.*

Jesus explained that not only is that how he and the Father relate to one another, but it is his hope for all of us that we would get to share that same intimacy. Jesus said in the Book of John:

"I do not ask for these only, but also for those who will believe in me through their word, that they may all be one, just as you, Father, are in me, and I in you, that they also may be in us, so that the world may believe that you have sent me. The glory that you have given me I have given to them, that they may be one even as we are one, I in them and you in me, that they may become perfectly one, so that the world may know that you sent me and loved them even as you loved me."[41]

That's the kind of God who created the heavens and the earth. He's not an isolated, lonely singularity. Neither is he three disconnected, separate Gods. God is three persons so intimate that they share sub-

---

41   John 17:20-23, ESV

stance with one another and their substance is indivisible. Then God said, "I'm going to make humanity in my own image. However, they will never fully understand some of the things I want to explain about myself unless I make it possible for them to experience a bringing together of their substance into one substance without losing their distinguishable personality." So when God was creating humanity, in order to communicate something of this miracle of intimacy, he created a physical manifestation of his own divine Spiritual nature, patterning our sexual intimacy on the unity in intimacy of God's own eternal spiritual being—the sharing of substance and life without losing the essential personality that is involved.

Marriage was intended by God to reveal that miracle. The language of sex and marriage reflects this same idea of intimate connectedness: "For this reason a man will leave his father and his mother and be united to his wife and the two shall become one flesh."[42] The idea of sex is the idea of this *perichoresis* of intimacy, of being in one another so that the two become one. The language of intimate relationships is the language of *perichoresis*, which is the language of God's own divine nature.

God uses sexual terms to explain spiritual truths

God has revealed something of himself and the wonder of his divine spiritual nature in the creation of human sexuality. In the Careforce Lifekeys program *The Search For Intimacy*, I unpack this topic in much more detail.[43] It's amazing to see in the Bible how often God uses sexual terms to explain spiritual truths. For example, when Jesus wanted to explain salvation, He said, "You've

---

42   Genesis 2:24
43   Information on Careforce Lifekeys programs can be seen at www.careforcelifekeys.org.

got to be *born* again."[44] When he wanted to explain how a person becomes a believer by the Word of God, he used the Greek word *sperma*, which means *seed*. He said, "If anyone becomes a child of God, he can't stay the same as he used to be because God's *sperma* abides in him and the DNA of His Word will be like sperm in him, and it will give him a brand new nature."

Another example of God using sex to convey spiritual insight was when he wanted to enter into a covenant relationship with Abraham, and this he did through circumcision. Now, I believe this is absolute proof that the Bible is divinely inspired, because I cannot imagine Abraham waking up one day and saying, "You know, boys, I have a brilliant plan. Let's start a new religion where we all cut off our foreskins. Good idea, eh? Everyone who wants to be circumcised form a straight line behind me." That's going to be a very short line! No man ever thought circumcision would be a great idea.

So you have got to ask yourself: *What is that all about?!* Well, God created our physical anatomy to reveal spiritual truths. When the foreskin was cut away, God was saying, "I want intimacy that is not clothed in flesh. I want to have intimacy with you that is heart-to-heart. I don't want intimacy with you that is constrained by your own flesh. I want a naked and open intimacy. That's the intimacy I'm looking for."

It is amazing how throughout the bible God uses sexual analogy over and over again. When Israel sought other forms of worship than love for Yahweh, he described the nation as a harlot[45]. When Israel walked faithfully with him, he called her a virgin[46]. Jesus calls the Church his bride. He calls himself the bridegroom, while the second coming of Jesus Christ is called a wedding feast.

44 John 3:3
45 Revelation 17:1,2
46 Lamentations 2:13

God created the idea of sex

God created sex to reveal so much to us. You and I were created from intimacy. God didn't create us because he was lonely and needy. He created us because he is thrilled with intimacy and chose to share it with us. He created us *out of* his intimacy. God got the idea for sex from his own divine, eternal, spiritual intimacy, and we have been created *for* it. We have not only been created *out of* intimacy, but we have been created *for* intimacy. In fact, intimacy is where eternity is headed:

Husbands, love your wives, as Christ loved the church and gave himself up for her… "Therefore a man shall leave his father and mother and hold fast to his wife, and the two shall become one flesh." This mystery is profound, and I am saying that it refers to Christ and the church.[47]

The Bible says that every marriage ceremony is a picture of eternity, where Jesus comes back and gathers His people together like a bride. This is also talking about Christ and the Church. The Bible also states: "Let us rejoice and exult and give him the glory, for the marriage of the Lamb has come, and his Bride has made herself ready; it was granted her to clothe herself with fine linen, bright and pure."[48] The physical expression of intimacy between a husband and wife is typical of the spiritual intimacy for which we have been created and will experience for all eternity.

We were created for two kinds of intimacy. You and I have a cry for two kinds of intimacy within us. The first is for spiritual intimacy with the God for whom we were created. St. Augustine put it this way: "You have made us for yourself, and our hearts will

47   Ephesians 5:25, 31-32, ESV
48   Revelation 19:7-8, ESV

know no rest until they find their rest in you!" One of the biggest challenges for you and me to get our head around is appreciating what true intimacy with God might really be like. Our current experience of spiritual intimacy is insufficient to fully appreciate what that might mean. Whether you have experienced it to any great degree or not, the fact is that we were made for our inner most being to be connected and joined with God's being, and for that amazing intimacy to give us a sense of fullness, safety and connectedness—a level of intimacy that would makes us realize that our life is secure, and provide a foundation for every other relationship.

The second cry for intimacy is that we were also designed for physical and emotional intimacy. While intimacy is expressed and experienced at many levels in forms such as family and friendship, sexual intimacy is the highest physical counterpart of spiritual intimacy. Both forms of intimacy are important in a healthy life. God built our physical sexuality on the model of spiritual intimacy, the ability of one spirit to be joined to another, and when those two spirits come together, life flows from one to the other.

The power of sex

Probably the greatest insight about sex that I have had from the Bible is the recognition that sex is so potent because God created our physical sexual capacities out of the pattern of His ability to bring two spirits intimately together and for life to flow between the two of them. Our society doesn't fully understand that. Society certainly understands that there is something extraordinary about our sex drive, and that there are deep and lasting repercussions if you mismanage your sex drive. For example, we know that if you touch a child sexually inappropriately, that child can be wounded for the rest of his or her life. That's why the law courts take the issue so seriously, even though it would be hard for the average individual to fully explain why a touch of that nature would so profoundly impact a child. It demonstrates that sex is extraordinarily powerful—for blessing and for harm.

I played Australian Rules football for many years, and so I know from experience that there can be a lot of physical contact on the field. Sometimes football matches are quite brutal places. The players bash into each other, kick, elbow, jab and pull—and they even throw the occasional punch. But at the end of the game, everyone shakes hands or hugs each other and they walk off to have a drink and say, "Good game, mate. No worries about the knocks and bruises. It's all good." The dressing room or the club house may be full of guys with broken knuckles, swollen cheekbones and black eyes from punching each other in the face during the game, but straight after the game they're all having a drink together.

I've encountered plenty of physicality—even violence—in sports matches, and yet it seems the long-term repercussions for the players are pretty minimal. The altercations with each other are like water off a duck's back, but not so in the area of our sexuality. It's interesting that nobody I've ever talked to walked away from their physical experiences on the football field wounded for the rest of their life, and yet one inappropriate sexual encounter can impact a person's life for 50 years.

I was in Phoenix, Arizona, speaking in a church one night about this same topic and a number of people came up for prayer at the end of the talk. As I made my way along the line of people gathered for prayer, there was a lady aged in her seventies standing there. I took her hand and I said to her, "Ma'am, how can I pray for you tonight?" She began by saying, "When I was 15 years old..." But then she had to stop, because big tears began to roll down her face.

As I held her hand I thought to myself, *It was a long time ago when she was 15 years old, but it's as painful for her tonight as it was all those years ago!* That's the extraordinary power of sex.

There is a power in sex that our society doesn't fully understand. However, what society today *does* understand is sexual abuse of children. There is hostility in our communities towards sexual abuse of children, because we have got that one figured out. We have seen enough of it to know for sure that when adults take advantage of children to meet their own sexual desires, they leave a destructive heritage that goes on for generations. Our communities are rightly angry about that. But what they do not understand is *why* sex is so powerful.

Society today thinks it has finally figured out some solutions to sexual problems. The consensus today is that if you get to the age of 15 or 16 and you are willing to have sex and you use a condom, well there can't be any possible harm in that! But the Bible tells us that we must understand where sex came from, and that sex is invested with a power that demands we guard it well.

1 Corinthians 6:13-20 tells us:

The body is not meant for sexual immorality, but for the Lord, and the Lord for the body. By his power God raised the Lord from the dead, and he will raise us also. Do you not know that your bodies are members of Christ himself? Shall I then take the members of Christ and unite them with a prostitute? Never! Do you not know that he who unites himself with a prostitute is one with her in body? For it is said, "The two will become one flesh." But he who unites himself with the Lord is one with him in spirit.

Flee from sexual immorality. All other sins a man commits are outside his body, but he who sins sexually sins against his own body. Do you not know that your body is a temple of the Holy Spirit, who is in you, whom you have received from God? You are not your own; you were bought at a price. Therefore honor God with your body.

There are a number of critical truths in that passage. First, verse 16 says that if you bring your body together with a prostitute, you both become one body. But then the very next verse says, "Don't you understand that when you receive Jesus, you become one spirit with him?" Placing those two thoughts together, side-by-side underlines the fact that sexual intimacy is the counterpart of spiritual intimacy. Anyone who has had a relationship with Jesus for any period of time can tell you that something begins to change. You look back and find it is truthful to say, "I'm a different person now. Over the years, Jesus has drawn near to me and he has joined himself to me. As a result, I now think differently, I feel differently, and I have different passions and desires. I have become a different human being through that intimacy with Jesus."

That's where God got the idea for sex. That's why when sexual intercourse takes place, it can leave a mark on a person that doesn't go away just because the two bodies part and go their own ways. The Bible tells us that every other sin you commit is outside your body.[49] No other sin you can commit has the impact within you that sex can have. Sex is unique because of where it came from. When you bring two bodies together in intimacy, those bodies are changed and those personalities are changed. That's why misused sexuality causes such long-lasting damage—because sex changes you.

The purpose of sex

It is for that reason that God surrounds sex with covenantal commitment. Our sexuality is inherently powerful, so it must be managed responsibly. In order to manage our sexuality responsibly,

---

49   1 Corinthians 6:18

we must understand its purpose, and then seek to make sure we are using it for the right purpose. So what is the purpose of sex?

1. **First, sex is designed by God for union.** That's why premarital intercourse is such a bad idea. As a youth pastor, the first person I ever counseled was a young girl who had been having sex with her boyfriend prior to marriage. Just a couple of months before the wedding, he dropped her and went off and married someone else. So she ended up in my office. She kept saying to me, "I don't seem to be able to let go of him!"

    I prayed for her and encouraged her that God had forgiven her, and sent her home. However, she came back again for another session only to say the same thing: "I don't seem to be able to let go of him!"

    I wasn't sure what she was trying to explain to me. I wondered if maybe it was some kind of demonic spiritual problem. So I prayed for release with all the authority I could muster and sent her home again. However, she came back again with the same concern, "I don't seem to be able to let go." What this young lady was saying to me, in effect, was, "Something's happened to me. I have been changed and I don't know how to undo what has been done inside."

    God designed sex to bring two people into union. Two people come together with different personalities and different backgrounds to share their bodies, bedrooms and their lives with all the diverse challenges that life can bring. Sex is designed to link people, join them together and change them in the process to last a lifetime. That's why we need to ensure that we don't link ourselves with people we have no intention of remaining faithful to for the rest of our lives. Sex changes you.

2. **Second, sex is for bonding.** Sex is glue. If only young people understood that one of the greatest privileges of marrying without a series of prior sexual relationships is that sex glues us to someone for a lifetime. For this cause a man will leave his father and his mother and *stick* to his wife, or glue himself to his wife. Sex is designed by God as a bonding experience.

I think this is one of the loveliest things about sex. At the time of writing, I have been married for almost 40 years. It has been by the grace of God that my entire sexual experience has been with the one woman. It's one thing for which I am profoundly grateful. I guess it wasn't for lack of desire that during my teenage years, when I didn't have a moral code that would have guarded me, God kept me for the one woman in my life. For nearly 40 years I have been stuck to that woman, and I love her more today than I ever did when I first married her. The Bible says, "For where your treasure is, there your heart will be also."[50] Maybe it's because I've spent so much money on her that that's where my heart is. (That's just a joke!) But the truth is that God designed sex to be a sticking factor.

It's important to say that when sex is not functioning as glue in a marriage, it can turn to dynamite and blow a couple apart. It is my prayer that as you read this book, God will help you to heal your relationship if it's been broken. I'm glad to say that many men have reported that the Valiant Man experience brought healing to the sexual relationship in their marriage.

3. **Third, God gave sex to us for the purpose of intimacy.** The Bible says, "Now Adam knew Eve his wife, and she conceived and bore Cain."[51] Sex is designed by God to help two people

50   Luke 12:34
51   Genesis 4:1, ESV

truly know one another. My friend, if you are married then truly knowing your wife has got to be one of the greatest goals of your life. Your sexual relationship is intended to provide an opportunity to draw both of you physically and emotionally close and truly know them. Again, my prayer for you is that this book will expose things that have prevented the experience of true intimacy in your relationship and bring healing to both of you.

4. **The purpose of sex is for procreation.** Sex isn't simply for us to have fun, although fun is part of the deal. God desires to use sex to create and to make you into a family. God said to Adam and Eve, "Be fruitful and increase in number; multiply on the earth and increase upon it."[52]

5. **The purpose of sex is revelation.** God wants to explain things to you about eternity and about heaven for which there are no words. For example God says, "I want you to come to me with a circumcised heart". What on earth does that mean? Circumcision is the removal of the foreskin of the penis. Once the foreskin is removed there is no guardian of flesh; the penis is exposed for every act of intimacy. That becomes a revelation of what God is looking for in your relationship with him. God wants you to come to him with your heart open and transparent, not clothed in flesh. There are many spiritual insights that would be incommunicable if sex did not exist. Sex exists to give a language to spiritual things that would otherwise be a mystery beyond understanding.

6. **The purpose of sex is pleasure and comfort.** I'm stunned at

---

52   Genesis 9:7

the way in which sexual intimacy has the power to pour the oil of comfort on a human heart. In a world where there is so much hurt, trouble and pain, sex has the ability to comfort and relieve some of the pain of life. Later in this book we will examine some of the biochemistry of sexual intimacy which underlines the fact that God deliberately designed sex to bring pleasure and comfort.

7. **The purpose of sex is healing.** Sexual intimacy can bring forgiveness that washes away mistakes and restores full and total acceptance of one another. The power of sexual intimacy causes forgiveness to be sealed. In family life there will always be tensions and conflicts that have the ability to pull you apart. God wanted sexual intimacy to reconfirm the fact that we are bonded together in family. The biochemistry of sex underlines God's commitment to our healing and well-being. Endorphins and enkephalins released in sexual intimacy reduce physical pain and promote healing, so much so that a happily married man lives nine years longer than his single counterpart— and it doesn't just *feel* longer! (That's another joke!)

8. **God gave us sex for discipleship.** Sex and marriage are among the greatest discipleship tools in life. While sex is endowed with a powerful potential for pleasure it also demands that we learn the difficult skill of containing our own desire and the pursuit of personal pleasure in circumstances where acting on our desires will curse rather than bless. Sex is a gift that will require us to learn how to do life like a child of God. Sex presents us with challenges designed to train us in the character of God. In taking the challenge of the discipleship of your sexuality seriously you can discover one of the greatest breakthroughs in your life. It is my prayer that this book will help in that process.

The impact of the 'God factor' on our sexuality

God's presence in the Garden of Eden meant that the first man and woman encountered each other in an atmosphere of emotional wholeness. The demands of their sex drive were mitigated by their experience of the deepest sense of divine love; they were already accepted, valued and had secure in their place of belonging. Sex was not a necessary prop for their self-esteem or their one hope at finding a moment of bliss.

One of the saddest things about this broken world is the reality that so many people live disconnected from God. They feel the emptiness and think it's about sex, but it's not about sex at all, it's about missing the deep and intimate love of God. The emptiness so many people feel is the result of not knowing that they are somebody in God's eyes, that they are valued by God. Without that emotional foundation people tend to rely on sex to fill the gaps. When a man expects a woman to provide for his complete fulfillment it is a huge and impossible challenge for her to bear.

The impact of the 'God factor' on our sexuality is reverberating through our society today, though it goes almost totally unrecognized. The very moment Adam and Eve committed that first act of rebellion and broke their relationship with God, a shattering took place in the heart of mankind that has affected men and women down through the ages.[53] The very next verse in that passage in Genesis says, "Then the eyes of both of them were opened, and they realized they were naked; so they sewed fig leaves together and made coverings for themselves."[54]

We have been impacted by the loss of our intimacy with God to a depth that most of us have never realized. We have lived like this

---

53   Genesis 3:6
54   Genesis 3:7

all our lives. We don't know what it would be like to be living in the presence of God, where our hearts are radiantly full, where we feel dignified, upright, holy, and magnificently whole every moment of every day. We don't know what that feels like, because it has never been our experience. You and I have grown up in a broken world. That's why you and I need to appreciate that some of the emptiness and stress we feel in life can never be met through sexual encounters. Some of the inner needs for acceptance, value and belonging are confused with sexual needs. Attempting to fill our deepest needs for the love of God with sexual behavior only confuses and frustrates us further. Some of our deepest needs will only ever be met by a deeper sense of connection with God.

Now, I am not saying that if you really love God you will never have any problems with your sex drive. I am not saying that if you love God more you will never again have the pressure to masturbate, or that pornography will never again be attractive to you, or that you will never again feel drawn to a woman other than your wife. Not at all; what I *am* saying is that some of the longing that we seek to satisfy through sex is actually a deep, heartfelt cry for God, and you and I have no idea how deep that cry is. When life seems empty and painful, it's easy for sex to be used in an attempt to meet needs it was never designed to satisfy.

Men use sex in inappropriate ways

Dr. Archibald Hart says there are seven ways in which men tend to use sex in inappropriate ways.[55] Perhaps you will find yourself in this list. I know I do.

---

55   A. Hart, *The Sexual Man*, Word Publishing, 1994, p. 50.

1. **Men have a tendency to use sex as a tranquilizer to relieve tension and stress.** When men feel pressure and stress, they may respond with the thought, *If I can have an orgasm, I know I'll feel better afterwards, and I know I'll feel relieved of this stress.* Women have the responsibility in some homes to solve a man's insomnia night after night. If he can't sleep, he thinks he needs sex to be able to get to sleep. He thinks it will help him to relieve tension and stress.

    Now, it's true that sex does tranquilize, and that's part of the miracle of sex, but when stress relief becomes the goal of sex instead of intimacy and bonding with your wife, then sex is being used for the wrong purpose and it's not healthy. It could be destroying your relationship, not building it.

2. **Men sometimes use sex as an antidepressant or as a medication to relieve feelings of melancholy or self-pity.** Men frequently use sex as a way to alter their mood. Men who feel they have failed, that their life is too challenging, or who don't like themselves often turn to sex to fix those feelings. While at times we can only be grateful that in the arms of a loving spouse some of the pain of life can be relieved momentarily, there is the potential for the development of a distorted perspective when sex is used as an antidepressant.

3. **Men can use sex as a way of venting emotion.** It's not always easy for men to express themselves emotionally with words. In fact, for some men the reason they enjoy sex is because it's the only time they have a way to express deep feelings. They're not always sure how to say the right words or how to express their feelings in other ways, so they enjoy sex because it is a way of expressing deeply felt emotions. Unfortunately, sex is

also used by some men as a way of venting anger; they use sex to get release from uncontrolled energy.

4. **Men sometimes use sex to prove their masculinity and power, or to prove their worthiness, popularity or irresistibility.** Men tend to use sex inappropriately when they try to prove something. I promise you that this can be more frequent than you might first imagine. Men want to feel like they are real men. They want to feel masculine. They want to feel like they are the lion. And so they have sex to prove something. Men want to feel like they are in control, and they express it through sex.

5. **Men also use sex to dominate their partner.** A man may take advantage of a woman's sexual desires while meeting his own need in order to feel like he is in charge.

6. **Men often use sex is to prove they love their wife, especially when they are not able to express love and tenderness in other ways.** So sex becomes the only way they know to express tender love towards their wife.

7. **Men frequently use sex to seek sensation.** This last one is very common. A man believes that somehow in sex he can find all the joys of human existence. When a man goes down that pathway, hoping that through an amazing experience of sexual pleasure he will give meaning to his life, he places too much demand on the sexual experience. Sex cannot be the meaning of life. When a man comes to see sex as the meaning of life there will, over time, be a tendency to demand that sexual positions become bizarre, that language becomes crude,

and that actions become violent. When there is an unhealthy drive to experience more and more all too often the outcome is frustrating; he experiences less and less.

REFLECTION

Do you find yourself in any of those seven scenarios? The question for you is this: What are you trying to get out of sex? It's time for a real analysis, so be radically honest about your motives and seek to understand what it is you are trying to get out of your sexual relationship. If you are married, it will speak profoundly to the issue of how you are treating your wife and what your spouse is experiencing or not experiencing in this vital area of your relationship.

Don't despair, and don't beat up on yourself. Just make an effort to understand.

Perhaps it's time for you to make a genuine and permanent commitment to Jesus Christ as the foundation of your life. A relationship with God begins with the *awareness* that you need it. The next step is to *ask* him for a relationship. Some useful things to say to God in those moments are words like:

"I've made a lot of mistakes, God, and I'm sorry. Please forgive me. Thank you for being patient with me. Come into my life and show me how to trust you and walk with you. Jesus. Here I am. Take my life today and guide me from this day forward."

Chapter 5

The Cycle of Addiction

"The happiness of a man in this life does not consist in the
absence but in the mastery of his passions."
Alfred Lord Tennyson

"If you have made mistakes, even serious ones, there is always
another chance for you. What we call failure is not the falling
down but the staying down."
Mary Pickford

Like the Blues Brothers, we're on a mission from God. Unlike the Blues Brothers, our mission is the pursuit of personal purity as we each take the journey from good man to valiant man. If we're going to pull that off, we must address the issue of the cycle of addiction.

Addiction is a brain condition of "neurochemical tolerance". That may not mean much to you right now, but by the end of this chapter it will begin to make sense. Not only that, it will also give you some serious insight into the challenging pathway from good man to valiant man.

By its very nature, an addiction is cyclical, even at the level of a fractional addiction. That's why it's so important that you begin to understand what it is that pushes you towards addictive behavior. You may need to make some decisions about how to respond differently to temptations and stimulations in the future.

Behind every addiction there is a fundamental desire to feel wonderful and to avoid pain, whether emotional or physical. You see, whilst we were all created to live emotionally full and fulfilled, the tragedy is that to some degree every man is empty, hurting, thirsty or needy. The fact that we are *not* full most of the time sets us up for either a degree of emotional pain or physical pain. And it's that pain that draws us towards the first stage of the cycle of addiction: *discovery*. The pain of life, our emptiness and our unmet needs set us up for the discovery stage in a path towards addiction.

Ted Bundy was an infamous serial killer who was executed on January 24, 1989. As a thirteen year old Ted Bundy was working his way through some neighborhood trash cans when he came across pornographic magazines for the very first time. As he read the words and the ideas that were presented to his fresh, innocent mind, he discovered that pornography gave him a tremendous release from the feelings of emptiness and pain in his life. As you probably know, pornography has the ability to change a man's mood and give him a momentary thrill. He made a discovery that day; there was something in life that actually worked for him. *I don't have to stay bored or empty or full of pain*, he thought to himself. *I can feel brilliant! I can feel fantastic!* That was Ted Bundy's discovery at 13 years of age.

The problem, of course, is that the relief pornography provides never lasts. It doesn't fix you for life. After the relief comes the relapse and then normality sets in. The pain of life returns and, depending on what you did to get your relief, it may even return with increased pain. That's what happened with Ted Bundy. Because he was the son of religious parents, he judged his own delight in porn as morally defective. So after the relief was relapse, and when the pain returned it wasn't the same pain he had previously felt it was now increased by a level of shame.

It was the pain that set Ted Bundy up for the discovery stage in the first place. Of course, no man wants to live with a constant experience of pain, so he went back to drink at the well of pornography to find relief again. And, of course, after the relief came the relapse. Over a period of time he discovered that the pornography he was using wasn't providing the same thrills—he found porn had diminishing returns (neurochemical tolerance was kicking in), and each relapse was deeper than the last one. The pain that returned was a deeper pain, driving him back again to find more relief.

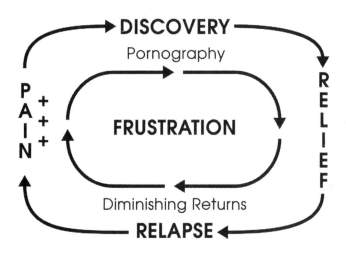

This is the cycle of addictive behavior. It starts with discovery and relief, then to relapse, and finally the pain returns, which brings a man back to drink at the same well, searching for relief again. Ultimately it results in frustration, and that frustration can drive a man to go to the next level of addiction. So often in sexual addiction that means upping the ante, going to a higher level of pornography, or going to a sexual expression that is even more daring, more dangerous and with greater consequences. That frustration tends to deepen the crisis over time.

The drivers of addiction in men

Well, that's a fairly simple overview of the cycle of addiction in general terms. It's a cycle waiting to capture every empty, pain-filled heart. All it requires is the first moment of discovery to get the cycle going. It can happen with alcohol, drugs, success, the approval of others… and, of course, sex. It helps to see the pointlessness of it all; the pain leads to short-term relief, which leads to relapse and often more pain... So what is it that drives men to seek relief through addiction? What are the drivers of addiction at work in a man's life that can cause him to go looking for pornography, masturbation, a fantasy life, or some other form of sexual addiction?

Boredom: The first one we need to confront is boredom. The ordinariness and the emptiness of life is a powerful driver towards addiction, especially for a man. Men are testosterone-driven. It is the defining hormone of manhood. Testosterone, as I've mentioned previously, is the hormone of daring, risk and aggression. A man is wired for a life that is thrilling. He hopes that life will be exciting, full of fun and adventure. The reality is that much of life is not thrilling, especially when responsibilities such as children, a job and a mortgage kick in. Life has a lot of normality and ordinariness attached to it. As we saw earlier in the introduction, King Solomon is *Exhibit A*—proof that even people in very exciting and exalted positions in life eventually come to feel that life is really quite ordinary.

Now, I think I live a fairly exciting life. I get to travel quite a bit and I do a lot of very interesting things, and yet I still feel my life is pretty ordinary at times. I wouldn't be surprised if you feel that way too. If you do, join the party. We discussed King Solomon in the Introduction but his story is so significant its worth visiting again. Even a guy like King Solomon felt bored at times. Here was a guy who was the King of Israel. He was the top-of-the-heap man. He was the richest guy in the world. There was nothing King Solomon did not have the authority to do. He ran the nation of Israel at a time when it was at its pinnacle. He could have had anything he wanted, but look at what he said: "My entire life is meaningless."[56] If it can happen to a guy like him, then none of us are exempt.

---

56   Ecclesiastes chapters 1 and 2

It's possible that Solomon lay awake at night pondering, *I get up in the morning, I put on my crown, I do my kingly work, build a city, solve a crisis, the sun goes down, I have an evening meal, I go to sleep, I wake up the next morning, and I do it all over again!* What is your life like? If you're anything like me, you wake up in the morning, travel to work, earn some money, return home, pay the bills, mow the lawn, watch the weeds grow back, watch the bills keep coming... There is a lot of ordinariness and repetition about life.

Because King Solomon was a man, he found that hard to live with. Men find boredom hard to live with. In Ecclesiastes Chapter 2 you find him going on a search for thrills. He tries entertainment, booze, money, big business... He even builds a pool in the backyard. Then he starts to buy things that nobody else can afford. Finally, it comes down to one of the biggest issues for men: sex- for King Solomon, it's a harem! Here is a guy who had 300 wives and 700 concubines. I take my hat off to him, because I have no idea where he got the energy for that kind of stuff. But, this guy had everything in life, and yet he found himself driven to experimentation and searching for something new to make his life thrilling.

If you don't want to get caught in a cycle of addiction, you have to confront the fact that much of life is supposed to be ordinary. You see, one of the solutions to men escaping the cycle of addiction is to have realistic expectations about life. My friend, God has designed you for a degree of boredom. The brain chemistry involved in addiction is better managed when you have low periods in your life in which you give areas of your life time to recover. If you don't do that, you will pay a big price.

Archibald Hart, author of the book *The Sexual Man*, calls this "camel travel". Mankind was designed for camel travel. In other words, life needs to have periods that are lived slow and gentle. But these days we are often damaged by the pace and the intensity of life. This is one of the great keys to becoming a *valiant man*—recognizing your masculine tendency to be driven constantly toward excitement, and deciding to resist it and embrace the normality of life; committing one's self to slow down at times and just enjoy the *normal* aspects of family, church, work, recreation and being alive.

It will take a deliberate decision to avoid filling every hour of every day with another big thrill. Be prepared to relax a little and take life a little slower. Be a little less intense, and be prepared to have some down time, some boredom periods, and some low moments because they are very healing. You may find yourself saying, *I've got to get more thrills in my life! I've got to do more, be more, experience more and challenge more!* But when you look at Solomon's experience, he makes a very important statement in Ecclesiastes chapter 2: "I hated life."[57] After he had pursued it all, he hated his life. If you try to counter the normality of life through sex you will end up hating your life too; and the people closest to you, like your wife and your kids, will end up hating their lives as well. Recognize that at least a degree of boredom and ordinariness is a normal element of the rhythm of life; so just accept life for what it is.

Unfulfilled needs: The second driver of addiction in men is unfulfilled needs. You and I were created to have certain needs met, and sometimes they are not met. Unmet needs in a man's life make him thirsty. The creation of the Valiant Man program was the concluding portion of my doctorate and, as such, required statistical analysis in the form of a pretest and post test. At the time of launching the pilot program, on which this book is based, 130 men signed up to do the 10 week journey. Of those 130 men, 124 completed a pre-test of 100 questions. This provided a window

---

57   Ecclesiastes 2:17

into the feelings, attitudes and experiences of more than 120 men. Statistics from the Valiant Man pre-test confirm what we have all suspected—that even amongst good men there are some deeply felt unmet needs. We need to find ways of dealing with that. To avoid going down the pathway of sexual addiction you need to understand that not all of the unmet needs in life can actually be met by sex.

Jesus once met a Samaritan woman who was attempting to fill the emptiness in her life through sex. She had been married five times, and at the time Jesus met her she was shacked up with a guy to whom she was not married. In his encounter with this woman, Jesus gave us an insight into a core issue at the back of addictive behaviors. Jesus was convinced that her particular need required a spiritual solution. Now, as I've already stated, I'm not trying to tell you that all your unmet needs will go away if you love God more, read your Bible more, and worship him more. But in the Samaritan woman's case, she was trying to meet an unmet need for intimacy with God by pursuing men. A relationship with God and a sexual relationship both centre on the cry for intimacy. You can fool yourself into believing that if you could just get more sex you would not have unmet needs in your life. This may be a surprise to you, but some of the needs in your life that you've identified as sexual needs may actually be about a cry for a deeper encounter with Christ and a deeper experience of God's presence. If that's true, then you are going to need to nurture a deeper intimacy with God.

Rather than condemning this woman's attempt to make life workable through sexual relationships, Jesus counseled her that she needed to return to a deep intimacy with God. This woman was trying to make sex more than it is, and there is a real temptation for men to do the same. However, sex is not the meaning of life! I've said it before, but we have to learn that lesson. We have to ensure that where there is an unmet need within us for intimacy with God, we don't try to meet it through sex. We have to ensure that we don't find ourselves being driven in that direction. If it rings true for you be honest about it and be prepared to say, *I think my life's getting out of control. I think I'm pushing this sex thing into areas that it was never intended to go.* Once you are honest about it, you can then begin to ask God for help, and he will help you.

Self-pity and anger: Two other drivers of addictive cycles are self-pity and anger. When you feel angry, hurt or misused, there is the danger that the emotional upset turns toward self-medication in terms of a self-justification for masturbation and pornography. So you will need to deal with self-pity and anger because it has the potential to drive you into addictive sexual behaviors as a release.

Childhood abuse: Another driver of addictive cycles is childhood abuse. We know that some perpetrators of sexual abuse have themselves been victims of sexual abuse. Sexual abuse distorts or twists sexuality, particularly so when abuse takes place in childhood. If the abuse is not addressed it can provide the potential for the abused to become an abuser, even if that abuse is self abuse.

The Valiant Man pretest and post test also addressed this issue. A question put to the pilot group was this: *To what degree do you believe your sexuality has been distorted by an experience of some form of sexual abuse?* We found that 34 % of the group believed sexual abuse had resulted in some level of significant distortion to their own sexuality. One of the reasons I have a passion to see the Valiant Man program offered more widely is that it gives men the opportunity to work through the damage and distortions that sexual abuse has caused in their lives. When men get help to process the impact of past sexual abuse in a healthy environment they protect themselves from ongoing harm and keep women and children safe from defective behaviors that could emerge later in life.

If this issue relates to you, I want to encourage you to take part in a Valiant Man program[58] to address the distortions of past abuse so that you can embrace your future with freedom in Christ.

Shame: One more reason why men are driven into addictive patterns is shame. A huge driver for addictive behavior is the pain of not liking yourself, feeling you're a loser, loathing yourself, and seeing yourself as unworthy.

Pre-test results show men's feelings about sex

The pilot program of Valiant Man gathered feedback from 124 participants to a range of questions about their sexuality. The men were asked to provide their answers to each question by choosing a number on a scale from 0 to 5; 0 being the lowest response and meaning 'Not Applicable or Least', and 5 being the highest response meaning 'Very Much or Most'.

What kind of men signed up for that course? They were ordinary guys, some of them were church-goers and some were not. One indication of the kind of men attending the course can be gauged from their answers to some of the questions. For example, I asked this question: *How important is it to you to manage sexual pressure in a way that God is honored?* Approximately 80% of the men chose 4 or 5 as their response to that question. This was a group of "good" men. So let's look through the window of the statistics I gathered and see what kind of struggles could be identified amongst a group of pretty ordinary Aussie men—a bunch of "good" men.

I asked the men: *How strongly do you associate feelings of shame with your sexuality?* The results showed that more than half of

---

58   Visit www.careforcelifekeys.org to discover where Valiant Man programs are being conducted.

the men indicated that there *was* a significant degree of shame impacting their sexuality. Another question I asked was this: *To what degree are unclean sexual thoughts causing you to feel separated from God?* Almost three-quarters of the men scored themselves at the high end of the scale.

When I asked this question: *To what degree are you disappointed with yourself over your failure to manage your sexuality?* More than three-quarters of the men told us that this was impacting significantly on their life. Most of the "good" men taking part in the program at that time were experiencing disappointment with themselves over their management of their sexuality, and those shame-based emotions are a great, big open door for addictive behavior patterns.

Another question was this: *To what degree do you feel unworthy to serve God because of your difficulty with sexual pressure in your life?* Just over half of the men answered with a 2 or higher, meaning that feelings of unworthiness were impacting significantly on their lives. Add that question to this one: *To what degree does your struggle with your sexuality damage your confidence as a man of God?* Three-quarters of the men answered 2 or higher. Again a significant issue not only for the men themselves, but for their families and the churches they are a part of. Men need help or their ability to be *eagles*—or spiritual leaders—is under serious threat. Concern about the responses to the two questions above is heightened by the fact that almost three-quarters of the men answered 2 or higher to this question: *How strongly do you feel God is disappointed in you because of your struggle with sex?* If we do not help men to resolve the crisis they experience over their sexuality, many of these "good" men will never become the *eagles* their families and their churches need them to be. So guys, we have to get help, and we have to help each other.

I'll mention just one more question. I asked: *To what degree is this true of you? "I wish I could break some of the sexual habits I have developed."* Over 70% of the men chose between 2 and 5 as their response. Most of the "good" men attending that course had a sense that they needed help to break habits—more than 60% of them felt this need strongly. Is there any doubt that men need help to become *valiant men*?

All of this adds up to the fact that *good* men experience significant levels of shame, and for many reasons we cannot leave the issue of shame unaddressed. The statistics demonstrate the need for the Valiant Man course, or its equivalent, and it underlines the importance of the issues we are seeking to address in this book. Masturbation, pornography and intrusive sexual fantasies are not only sexual behaviors, they also fuel our feelings of shame and these all add up to a destructive addictive cycle. We need to find solutions to that reality.

Feeling guilty is important

Now here's the deal: If you experience feelings of guilt over things you shouldn't be doing in your sexual behaviors, don't try to anesthetize or suppress those feelings of guilt, because appropriate guilt is one of the ways in which we accept responsibility; it's one of the motivations towards change. Guilt helps us to mend our ways. False guilt is not helpful, but appropriate guilt is vital to our humanity and must not be suppressed.

However, when a man has a blanket of shame about his sex drive in general, that shame has the power to fuel the very behavior from which he is seeking to escape. That's what turns a man into a neurotic and compulsive individual. You see, neurotic guilt causes a man to want to be punished and to *want* to feel bad, if he feels that's what he deserves. It causes a man to *not* want to be forgiven and *not* want to be healed as he feels he doesn't deserve forgiveness and healing.

Shame over being a sexual man and having a strong sex drive is just not helpful, nor is it necessary. When fear and shame join hands, all too often the outcome is denial and silence. Unfortunately, many of us have responded with both denial and silence. They have become part of our lives.

Now, if you're going to deal with shame, it's important to find out what the Bible really says about sexual behavior. Heaping shame on yourself for something that God isn't really that concerned about is not helpful. Part of building a healthier life is to get rid of shame simply because it helps drives the addictive cycle. That doesn't mean deciding something is okay when God says it isn't, but every one of us needs to learn to live under amazing grace if the destructive work of shame is to be successfully addressed. A man can find his sex drive disturbing if he is unable to live with the sense that God knows and understands the battle. After all, Jesus himself had all the masculine equipment and lived with testosterone too. He felt the same passions and urges yet the Bible says that he handled all of that without sin. The Bible says he was tempted in all the same ways we have been tempted, so Jesus understands our struggles because he himself has faced them.

The Bible and masturbation

Masturbation can be a huge source of shame, fueling further pain and thus reinforcing addictive behaviors of various kinds. I spoke to a man who could identify his entrance into the drug scene at the age of fifteen as an escape from the pain of shame emanating from his encounter with masturbation which began at the age of eleven. If you want a litmus test for the shame level involved in masturbation just try bringing it up as a subject of casual conversation next time you are hosting a dinner party. Masturbation is a powerful shame producer, so it's important to know what the Bible actually has to say about masturbation — to see if the level of shame many men are living with is appropriate or not.

In studying this issue, you won't find the word listed in a Bible Dictionary—it just isn't a word that appears in the Bible. However, that doesn't mean the Bible has nothing to say about the issue. So let's explore a few passages that could be brought to bear on the subject.

Deuteronomy 23:10-11 says:

> If one of your men is unclean because of a nocturnal emission, he is to go outside the camp and stay there. But as evening approaches he is to wash himself, and at sunset he may return to the camp.

Have you had a wet dream? Here the Bible says, in effect, "Just go out and wash yourself and then come back again."

Leviticus Chapter 15 deals with the issue of an emission of semen. First, it talks about a situation in which a woman is involved, and then it refers to a situation where there is no woman involved. Here is what it says:

> When a man has an emission of semen, he must bathe his whole body with water, and he will be unclean till evening. Any clothing or leather that has semen on it must be washed with water, and it will be unclean till evening.[59]

That's the same instruction as the first passage which relates to a nocturnal emission. The very next verse goes on to say:

59   Leviticus 15:16-17

When a man lies with a woman and there is an emission of semen, both must bathe with water, and they will be unclean till evening."[60]

The editors of the International Standard Bible Encyclopedia suggest that the reference above in verses 16-17—"When a man has an emission of semen, he must bathe his whole body with water"—is, in fact, an instruction that refers to masturbation. We have a clear reference to a nocturnal emission in Deuteronomy 23:10-11, and in Leviticus 15:18 we have a clear reference to both a man and a woman being involved. So, in looking at verses 16-17, it would make sense to argue that the reference to an emission of semen—which is neither a nocturnal emission nor sexual intercourse where a woman is involved—is most likely dealing with a reference to masturbation. Not everyone agrees with that interpretation, but I think it has merit.

So what does the Bible have to say about masturbation? If the passage just referred to does not refer to masturbation, then there is no direct mention of the issue at all. However, if the passage above does refer to masturbation, the same instruction that is given to the man who has had sexual intercourse with a woman is given to the man who has had an emission of semen when there is no woman involved. The instruction to both of them is simply this: "Take a bath." The instruction to the man who has had a nocturnal emission, the man who has ejaculated without a woman involved, and the man who has had sexual intercourse are all considered unclean until the end of the day is basically this: *"Have a bath and go home."*

Cranking up the shame levels on masturbation to try to provoke yourself to change is really unhelpful. These passages of Scripture

60   Leviticus 15:18

reveal that an ejaculation without one's wife being involved is not as big a deal as some would like to make it.

This does not mean that masturbation is necessarily a healthy activity or that it is irrelevant to the development of *valiant manhood*. Later in this book we will look at the issue in greater detail. All I am seeking to establish at this point is the importance of clarifying the difference between guilt over behavior that is morally illicit... and shame-based emotions driven by false guilt over issues that are not significant. What we should be concerned about is not so much the act of masturbation as what is going on in the head and heart. What is the driver of masturbation in a man? What is his reason for masturbating?

Sometimes a man has such a build-up of semen it creates a pressure in his body that he has to deal with somehow. The married man may have the opportunity to resolve the pressure through sexual intercourse, yet even for the married man that is not always possible. A long period of geographical separation, illness, pregnancy, or any one of a number of other reasons can place a married man in the same position as the single man. What now?

Well, the second port of call can simply be to put up with it. For many, if not for most, this is the appropriate response—for reasons we will investigate later in the book. However, for some the relentlessness of sexual pressure can be so debilitating as to cry out for resolution. Origen, one of the heroes of the early church, found his libido such a distressing pressure that he decided to resolve the problem by cutting off his testicles. It underlines the extreme pressure that some men experience. I have to wonder if there is another less extreme option available to those for whom the pressure can go beyond unpleasantness to physical pain.

An option for some can be to masturbate to release the physical pressure. In some circumstances masturbation may be an appropriate release for a man. We should not automatically attach shame to every act of masturbation in order to try to force ourselves to change our behavior. If the Bible does not make ejaculation a big issue neither should we. Purity of heart and mind is the goal, and physical release of sexual pressure is not automatically associated with impurity of heart or mind. If it is, we have an issue—and we'll deal with this in greater detail later in this book.

At this point, however, it will be enough to say that if masturbation happens, avoid the complication of unnecessary shame. How do you do that? You turn from a shame-based response in your growth as a *valiant man* and begin to lean on God's amazing grace; know that God loves you and He is for you in the middle of your sexual pressure. It will become important for you to learn the true purpose of sex on your journey so that masturbation does not become a destructive element in your life—and it can! But for now, we start with grace, not shame. As we progress towards *valiant manhood*, we will set our sights on continuing to grow in self control so that we don't have to respond to every demand our body makes. A *valiant man* will need to get beyond the attitude that says, "Well, I suddenly had a sexual urge, so I had to satisfy it." It will become important that we learn to rule our own bodies, and as we learn to do that we'll be able to escape from distortions and undo the pressures that have been bugging our lives for years.

When we asked men taking part in the Valiant Man program questions about their feelings towards masturbation, 65% said masturbation had been a strong temptation and 67% said it had been a significant life problem. My friend, if you are in that category and masturbation has been a significant problem for you, I want to encourage you to try to approach it with a different mindset from now on. You see, you and I are pursuing purity, but "purity" built on a foundation of shame will not be purity at all. (We'll talk more about this later in the book.)

Having said all that, it may be that the beliefs, behaviors and experiences that have formed your sexuality are a closely guarded secret. It may be that you have never shared them with anybody, that you guard them as a secret because you are ashamed of them. Let me encourage you to break the silence. The Valiant Man program embraces a small group model committed to transparency and confidentiality. In that environment it is life-changing to find the courage to tell the truth. Silence is a form of darkness, and things that you feel ashamed about will tend to ooze from the darkness into other areas of your life and defile you. On the other hand, if you bring things out into the light and appropriately share them with close friends or your Valiant Man small group, the power of those secrets to tyrannize your life can be broken. When you bring secrets like that out into the light and say, "I want to share my story—this is how sex unfolded in my life," you will find freedom that will liberate you from those dark moments. Don't let shame rule your life, because it is one of the ways you get driven into addictive behavior patterns. Break the silence.

The chemistry of the cycle of addiction

It's not difficult to understand the cycle of addiction in terms of feelings and behavior: discovery leads to relief, followed by relapse, emptiness, pain returns, and so back to discovery again. However, it has become clear through years of intensive research that addictive behaviors are not merely emotional/behavioral cycles; they are also bio-chemically enforced.

What is an addiction? In recent years an addiction has been described as a brain disease, not just a behavioral disease. Dr. Alan

I. Leshner describes it well: "Addiction is a brain disease expressed in the form of compulsive behavior."[61] Perhaps the most informed definition of an addiction is simply "a condition of neurochemical tolerance". Through in-depth research on drug and alcohol addiction, we have come to better understand how the brain works. So let's take a brief look into the chemistry involved in the addictive cycle. First, we'll learn a little from the experience of addiction to drugs, and then we'll see how that informs our understanding of sexual addiction.

People take drugs because they want to feel good... and drugs work. There are three centers of the brain that are particularly related to the experience of pleasure or reward. One is called the VTA (the ventral tegmental area), another is called the nucleus accumbens and the third is the prefrontal cortex. They are designed to give pleasure in response to behaviors involved in actually living and relating in a real world—whether it be a kiss on the lips or eating an ice cream. An action or a relationship triggers a response, particularly in the nucleus accumbens, and feelings of pleasure or feelings of well-being are the result. However, when a drug such as heroin gets into the blood stream, it flows directly to the pleasure centers of the brain and stimulates them causing the brain to release the signal, "We're having fun here, aren't we?"— even though the body is not doing anything that would naturally cause that pleasure to occur.

Through the stimulation of the nucleus accumbens in your brain pleasure is experienced, no matter what that pleasure might be— whether sexual pleasure, the smell of coffee in the morning, the feel of sunlight on your body when you're out playing golf, or enjoying

---

61   I gratefully acknowledge Dr. Alan I. Leshner and his research for insights on addiction and brain processes.

the taste of flavored ice cream. Any pleasure that you experience in life is handled by the nucleus accumbens. Drugs such as heroin, nicotine and cocaine tend to go first to the prefrontal cortex, which then stimulates the nucleus accumbens. So getting pleasure from taking drugs comes down to the drugs we take pressing the button on that part of our brain called the nucleus accumbens, giving us the pleasure sensations we long to experience.

The fact is that drug addiction highjacks the reward pathway in our brains—a pathway which would normally only be triggered by actually *doing* something in the physical or emotional world, causing our brain to send out those pleasure signals even though no pleasure-giving behavior is actually happening.

Addiction takes place as we reach neuro-chemical tolerance. At this point the nucleus accumbens no longer gives out the pleasure signals it used to, demanding another fix or a greater fix before another burst of pleasure signals are released. The brain is so wired that regularly hammering the nucleus accumbens in an attempt to get big doses of pleasure signals results in the nucleus accumbens dialing itself down over time. When it reaches neurochemical tolerance, it requires a greater threshold of stimulation before the pleasure signals are experienced. It's as if the brain raises the high-jump bar and won't allow the pleasure signals to be experienced without an increase in input.

One of the side effects of the raising of the threshold of stimulation or the dialing down of the pleasure signals is the damage it does to our experience of all the smaller pleasures in life. As neurochemical tolerance is reached, the lesser stimuli—all of the lesser natural experiences of life that once gave you pleasure—no longer trigger the nucleus accumbens. As a result, the little pleasures in life begin to recede into the background and give you no pleasure at all. You wake up in the morning and the aroma of coffee no longer gives you the joy it once did. Holding your wife's hand no longer gives you the joy you once felt. That feeling of achievement after you've mown the lawn no longer exists. This is a condition known as *anhedonia*. In the search for a more exciting life we have managed to turn our whole world grey. It is this grey world that drives the addict onward and deeper into the addictive cycle in the search for pleasure that becomes harder and harder to find.

Welcome to the chemistry set inside your head

What does all this have to do with sexual addiction? Well, welcome to the chemistry set inside your own head. The drug addict or the alcoholic has to acquire his drug of choice from some outside source. The sex addict carries his chemistry set with him wherever he goes and makes his own. Sexual addiction messes with the chemistry set devoted to sexual arousal that resides right in your own head. There are over 300 different chemicals involved in the chemistry of your brain. Only about 60 of those 300 chemicals are well understood, and some of the most potent of all are dedicated to the experience of sex and sexual arousal.

Sexual arousal can be triggered by sight, touch, sounds, memories, fantasy and smell. Even your nose can get you into trouble. The vomeronasal organ is designed to detect pheromones—scents released in sweat—and carry the signals directly into the sexual arousal centers in the brain. Pheromones have the ability to cause a woman's menstrual cycle to become more regular, and to synchronize the man's testosterone levels to the woman's monthly cycle.

Of that cluster of chemicals dedicated to sexual arousal, perhaps the most potent of them all is phenylethylamine or PEA. PEA has been described by some as the sexual chemistry of novelty. The potential it has to be involved in the addictive process is signaled by the fact that its chemical construction is almost identical to crack cocaine. Dopamine, nor-epinephrine and especially phenylethylamine are all cousins of amphetamines. PEA released internally by the brain's own processes is mimicked by cocaine taken by the drug addict. Why would a person take cocaine? Simply because the experience it produces is one of near total euphoria—the feeling that you can fly, that your feet aren't touching the ground; you feel giddy with a sense of well-being. And who wouldn't want to feel like that—at least sometimes!

Why is PEA called the sexual chemistry of novelty? Because this chemical is usually triggered by someone with whom you're not familiar; it's at the centre of that experience we call 'love at first sight'. The fingerprints of PEA can be found all over love songs from every generation. Do you recognize this lyric:

One enchanted evening you will see a stranger, you will see a stranger across a crowded room, and somehow you'll know…

Here's another one:
I could have danced all night, I could have danced all night and still have asked for more…

That's the result of phenylethylamine. Someone triggers that explosion of cocaine-like brain chemistry and suddenly a drug trip with giddy feelings of euphoria has you on another planet. That's what happened to me as a young twenty two year old teacher checking in a bus load of senior school students departing for a week of adventure in Tasmania. Just the sight of one of those students getting on that bus triggered a reaction in me so strong and unexpected that for the next six days I was in danger of ruining my career, my marriage and my life. For six days it made me wonder if I'd married the wrong person. I hadn't; I was just temporarily insane with unexpected PEA upsetting my equilibrium. I had to deliberately hold on to what was right to survive—which I did.

My brain detoxified over time and I recovered my grip on reality. I'm so glad I didn't believe the message of that cocaine-like brain chemistry and destroy my marriage in the process.

Why would such chemistry exist in the human brain? I believe it was engineered into our biochemistry by our Creator, who knew that most marriages in history would not be marriages of romance but marriages of arrangement. Raised in a pure environment, the first time a man would see a woman naked would be on his wedding night—and PEA would act like kindling for a fire, bursting open a passion that would turn a relationship into a delight rather than an endurance contest. The honeymoon experience would be one of euphoria and giddy delight, founding the marriage relationship in a thrilling encounter.

However, this chemistry fades and gives way to the slower burn of other brain chemistry as the relationship becomes familiar. One of the great dangers of pornography is its ability to revisit the thrill of PEA by presenting sexual imagery which is unfamiliar—and PEA is the sexual chemistry of novelty. Watch the same stuff over and over and neuro-chemical tolerance sets in; new stuff and heavier stuff is required to stimulate the locus accumbens to get the same pleasure sensations; and the pathway to addiction is being trod. We have been given a profound pleasure potential in our sexual wiring, but with that gift comes the demand for a high level of moral responsibility and discipleship.

So PEA has the capacity to provide you with a huge thrill, but it will fade away. If you make the PEA experience the measure of a relationship, you'll only be able stay with someone long enough for the initial thrill to wear off, and then you'll find yourself no longer interested in that person; you won't be able to develop long-term relationships. Knowing this could save your life some day.

Then there's adrenalin. Adrenalin is the hormone of fight or flight. Add adrenalin to sexual arousal and it heightens or intensifies the experience. Adding adrenalin to the sexual experience is very exciting, but very, very dangerous. Paired with sexual arousal, it has the potential to become the basis of an addictive spiral resulting in distorted sexual experiences that move towards perversion. There is a real danger for a man when he tries to turn sex into the meaning of life—when he looks to sex to provide a consistent thrill so powerful that it justifies his existence. Sex is not the meaning of life, it is a delightful element of life. One dangerous discovery a man can make at some point in his life is the fact that a surge of adrenalin mixed with sexual arousal really does kick the experience into a more thrilling zone. It might happen, for example, when a man sees something a bit risqué, a little bit naughty, and—*boom!* That adrenalin lifts the intensity of the experience to a whole new level in his brain. The excitement can tempt him to try to repeat the experience in his own bedroom with pressure on his wife to allow a little porn into their entertainment or some perceived "naughtiness" in their sexual relationship. It is a dangerous pathway for many reasons. She will quickly perceive that she is being *used*, a defiling and demeaning experience for any woman. Then, as neurochemical tolerance kicks in and the level of thrill begins to return to normal, the pressure will be on to heighten the experience by more and more degrading behavior. Trying to make sex the meaning of life can kill a relationship.

It was this mix of adrenaline and sexual arousal that eventually turned Ted Bundy into a killer. The sense of naughtiness and guilt produced the adrenalin surge. And paired with pornography, the rising level of excitement made normal sexual arousal seem tame and insufficient. With each escalation of risk, danger and ultimately criminal behavior, the sexual thrill could be recaptured. But neurochemical tolerance would catch up, and the thrill would ultimately diminish, providing the impetus for new risks, new dangers and more debauched behavior. For Bundy, the cycle went all the way to pathological behavior.

Most men will never go that far. Fear and moral restraint will keep most men from pursuing sex across criminal boundaries, but a multitude of men have pursued the thrill of sex in such a way that it has led to distortions. Those distortions can ultimately overwhelm what once was a good marriage. In another chapter we'll talk about what it takes to recover that normality, but for now it's enough to simply acknowledge and identify the problem.

Now, let's look at the impact of endorphins and enkephalins in your body. Endorphins and enkephalins are natural opiates. The beautiful thing about these substances is that you tend to experience them more in a long-term relationship. Once a man and a woman have been together and have learned to make their sexual experience beautiful, more opiates and enkephalins are released. Those natural opiates influence the brain by relieving pain and giving a profound sense of well-being. Its good sex with the same person that brings the endorphins and the enkephalins into play and it is part of what can make a marriage wonderful.

Sexual intimacy is intended by our Creator to be part of the emotional and physical healing processes in the body. You may have heard a bad joke about marriage that goes something like this: "Married men live longer? No, mate, it only feels longer!" The fact is that on average a happily married man lives nine years longer than his single counterpart. It doesn't just *feel* longer, it really *is* longer. Part of that phenomenon is the impact of those endorphins and enkephalins as they do their healing work in our bodies. You don't have to make sex the meaning of life—just let sex be what it is and you'll be the better for it.

The key hormone in sexual arousal, however, is testosterone. Testosterone is the passion hormone in both men and women.

However men live with testosterone levels that are 20 times higher than those of women. The result is that men tend to have a relentless sex drive that at times can be somewhat disturbing to a woman. Testosterone is the defining hormone of masculinity. Our brains have been re-wired by the action of testosterone in the womb, and our brains respond constantly to its action.

Women are not defined by testosterone. Their hormonal engine results in widely divergent levels of desire for sexual intimacy. This calls for significant levels of personal restraint and consideration on the part of the average man. Learning to manage this testosterone fog is part of the challenge for every *good* man wanting to become a *valiant* man.

We can't complete this brief introduction to the bio-chemistry of passion without saying something about oxytocin. Oxytocin has been described as the "cuddle hormone". This hormone gives an emotional sense of *bonding* or *belonging*. A desire for belonging is one of the deepest inward desires in the human heart, so moments in which a deep sense of belonging is *felt* are moments that provide deep satisfaction and peace in the human soul. Since oxytocin gives that felt experience of belonging and bonding, every *valiant man* should know what can release it in his wife. By the way, since oxytocin works most potently in the presence of estrogen, it does its work better in women than men. Oxytocin is released by touch and by closeness, by breast feeding, and in massive quantities in childbirth. It is designed to stick people together.

While we're on the subject of touch, it's important for a man to know that a woman has ten times the number of touch receptors in her skin than he does. The touch of a man is designed to cause a woman to feel close and connected to him. That's one reason why fathers need to be affectionate toward their daughters; hugging helps create that sense of belonging which they so deeply need and makes them less vulnerable to the touch of some guy who does not have their destiny or best interests at heart. To caress your wife, hug her and touch her non-sexually—with tenderness and gentle affection—often is nothing less than benign self interest. A woman is designed by God to respond to touch. A man is designed to respond to sight. While physical touch stimulates oxytocin and a sense of belonging, sexual intimacy has the potential to release a veritable flood of oxytocin with its wonderful after-glow of felt bonding and a deep sense of belonging. The *valiant man* knows this and deliberately guards those precious moments during and after sexual intimacy to allow the joy, peace and pleasure of belonging to heal, restore and knit two hearts together for life.

You see, marriage was designed by God around a certain kind of pleasure bond. Every one of us needs to know that sex is glue. Sex was designed to stick things together. This is what is known as orgasmic programming. In his book *Holy Sex*, Terry Weir says, "Whatever fantasies or images your brain is focused on at the point of orgasm becomes programmed into your memory with great erotic power."[62] This is why sex is glue. When God said, "For this reason a man will leave his father and mother and be united to his wife,"[63] God backed that up with a range of neurochemical transmitters designed to make the bond a source of delight and a well of emotional and physical healing.

You were created to be addicted to your wife

If only society would co-operate with the Creator, we would discover that we have been designed to experience the miracle of

---

62 T. Weir, *Holy Sex*, Whitaker House, 1999, p 241.

63 *Ephesians* 5:31

a growing *addiction* to one woman—the one we marry. The thrilling power of PEA has been designed to awaken love in our soul during the process of courting, only to explode on that first night of naked intimacy. Sexual intimacy and physical closeness during the honeymoon is intended to release wave after wave of oxytocin, bringing a sense of felt belonging to mark the heart for a lifetime. That sense of belonging can be renewed with every touch of the hand and every tender moment throughout life. As the furious fire of PEA subsides into the steady glow of tender companionship, the chemistry of endorphins and enkephalins brings healing, renewed strength and restored emotions through all the challenges of life. In the process, we build a loving relationship and learn to know one another and care for one another. God designed our sexuality around elements that work in harmony to stick a man and a woman together for life - through all the difficulties and challenges life can throw at them. My friend, if this has not been your past, you need to know it can be your future.

However, sex can also stick you to the wrong things. A man who has been doing pornography may find that feelings begin to stir in him when he drives past a certain store. Or he begins to have feelings stirring in him when he gets close to a computer terminal. Or he feels stirred when he walks into a hotel bedroom and sees the television set in the corner and he knows it shows pornographic programs. These are environmental cues that have stuck sex together with certain behavior patterns and work to make them addictive.

Sex is like glue, which is one of the reasons why a sexual addiction may not be broken alone. You may need to embrace a commitment to accountability to others—to people who are committed to helping you unstick yourself. In sexual addiction, alcohol addiction and drug addiction, environmental cues continue sending signals long after you have decided you don't want to be an addict any more. That's why it will be important to have someone else to keep you honest; your buddies will not be affected by the same cues that you are.

Sex was created as a bonding experience. God intended it to glue a man and a woman together for life. It can work legitimately or illegitimately. It can cause you to be glued in your marriage. It can cause you to be glued to a fantasy life. It can cause you to be glued to pieces of paper in the form of pornography. It can cause you to be glued to unhealthy masturbation. It can cause you to become glued to prostitutes or an endless search for another phenylethylamine high.

When you move into the experience of sexuality, you begin to deal with a very powerful chemistry set right there in your own head. A look, a sound, a touch, a smell or an idea can trigger a chemical reaction more powerful than you can imagine. It may be that in your own experience much of that chemistry has been misused in the past. But don't despair. *Good* men can become *valiant* men. If you have the willingness, the humility and the courage to continue reading, the best is yet to come!

REFLECTION

Sexual addiction is real and it is dangerous. But I want to encourage you that purity is worth fighting for it and it is worth guarding. The pathway to sexual addiction is not a pathway to endless pleasure, it is a pathway to frustration and damage. If you are aware that you've begun to walk down the pathway of fractional addiction, or if you are experiencing genuine sexual addiction in some form, there are some steps you are going to have to take:

+ Don't deny or repress the truth—face it.
+ Stop trying to make sex the meaning of life.
+ Make the cultivating of long-term loving relationships your highest priority.
+ Turn your eyes away from "junk" sex experiences.
+ Destroy all your pornographic material.
+ Identify the cues that trigger habits. (We'll talk more about this in future chapters.)
+ Decide to be accountable. So break the silence, and tell the truth about your struggle to someone you can trust.

Because of the abuse of the pleasure and reward pathways that may have occurred in your brain, the cellular changes that take place in the brain can last for weeks, months and even years after the behavior has changed. It will take courage and persistence to retrain your brain, but be sure of this: your efforts will have their reward.

Chapter 6

The Understanding Man

"A good husband makes a good wife."
John Florio

"Men and women belong to different species, and
communication between them is a science still in its infancy."
Bill Cosby

Actor Mel Gibson played the leading man in the 2000 movie *What Women Want*. Putting aside the deficiencies of the movie for now—in purely moral terms there were plenty—the film portrayed with poignancy and humor what it means to women when men take the trouble to understand their experience of life. When Mel found himself imbued with the capacity to know what women really and deeply wanted, he was transformed. He became one of that rare breed: the understanding man.

The beasts with four faces outlined in chapter one give us some insight into the qualities that make up the *valiant man*. First, he is to be an ox, which means he is to carry the burdens of his family. Second, he is to be a lion, protecting and guarding his family. Third, he is called to be an eagle; a man of God, a spiritual leader to his family and a man who relates to God in prayer and worship. Fourth, he is to be a man who understands his own humanity, his own passions and desires. This combination of all four faces is what you and I are aiming to become. Now, into that mix we add the challenge to become *an understanding man*.

When a man doesn't understand the complexity of a woman's sexuality, the potential for her to be wounded is very real. Compounded insensitivity can eventually train a woman to be defensive, touchy, and feel continually unsafe. Make that your woman's overall experience of life and neither of you will be happy. A man's ignorance, insensitivity and incapacity to understand her needs will teach her to guard and protect herself. In that environment, the joy of intimacy is impossible. Again, being an understanding man is nothing less than benign self interest. Yet beyond all issues of self interest, growing from being a *good* man to a *valiant* man calls for you to become an understanding man, where you learn to respect the much more complex nature of a woman's sexual wiring—for her sake. She was created to be thrilled and fulfilled in sexual intimacy, but this experience will be denied her unless you become *an understanding man.*

The male is clearly a simpler creature when it comes to the issue of sex. Sex for you and I can be easy, and it can be quick. All a man needs is an erection, a few brief moments, and his testosterone-driven sexuality is ready to go. In a few more moments he can be done and blissfully happy. The only time when this may not be the case is when he has just had an orgasm, which means that for a short period of time he is like a flat battery and his interest in sex might be somewhat subdued.

To take a cooking analogy, a man is like a microwave and a woman is like a crock pot. He can be sexually alert in seconds and fulfilled in minutes, but a woman needs time and appropriate circumstances to warm up and enjoy the miracle of orgasm. An understanding man will be blessed if he will give her the time she needs, because when she is ready she is amazing.

A woman is designed to delight in sex

I do not believe that human beings are the end product of evolutionary processes. Neither do I believe that the physiology and the biochemistry of sex is the end product of evolution. It is brilliant, it is complex, and it is the product of a crafted, thoughtful creative expression by a Creator who has revealed something of himself in the process. The intention and personality of our Creator is perceived not only in the words he inspired about sex in the Bible, but in the way in which he has created our bodies and souls. The existence of the clitoris is absolute proof that God intended woman to find deep pleasure in sexual intimacy.

Now, if you don't know much about the clitoris, you need to buy a book about it and read up on it. As I mentioned in chapter three, the basic template for every new fetus is the feminine pattern. The male penis develops from the same pleasure center that in a woman becomes the clitoris; stimulated by a chemical miracle that same structure develops into its masculine form. We know from our own personal experience that the penis is designed to give pleasure. Well, the feminine form of that same organ has been hidden internally in a woman's body, intended to give her an even greater experience of pleasure than it is possible for a man to experience. A full female orgasm is a marvel of delight beyond that which any man is capable of experiencing.

It is a tragedy that some cultures and some religions so fail to understand God's intention for sex that they actually destroy the clitoris in a woman through female circumcision. What they are doing is taking something that God intended to be a blessing to a woman and eradicating it. They have failed to appreciate that sex is not simply a man's preserve; it is also intended to be a woman's preserve. Not only is that clear in the way God created a woman's body—through the presence of the clitoris and its capacity to give a woman the experience of an orgasm—it is also clear through the evidence of God's Word.

Passages from the Song of Solomon attest to the fact that sex is really supposed to be an anticipated delight for a woman. Here are some biblical examples of sexual intimacy from a woman's perspective:

Let him kiss me with the kisses of his mouth—
for your love is more delightful than wine.[64]

How handsome you are, my lover!
Oh, how charming!
And our bed is verdant.[65]

His left arm is under my head,
and his right arm embraces me.

---

64 Song of Solomon 1:2
65 Song of Solomon 1:16. *Verdant* means "green with growing plants".

Daughters of Jerusalem, I charge you
by the gazelles and by the does of the field:
Do not arouse or awaken love
until it so desires.[66] [In other words, give love all the time it needs.]

Your lips drop sweetness as the honeycomb, my bride;
milk and honey are under your tongue.[67]

Milk and honey are under your tongue? Now, you have got to
ask yourself: How would he know that? Obviously this is not just
describing lip kissing; this is deep tongue kissing. The Bible understands that kissing can be done at various levels and different ways.
Here is a description of kissing that is so intimate that he can say,
"Milk and honey are under your tongue."

The writer continues:
You are a garden locked up, my sister, my bride.[68]

Then she responds:

Awake, north wind,
and come, south wind!
Blow on my garden,
that its fragrance may spread abroad.
Let my lover come into his garden
and taste its choice fruits.[69]

The Bible has this rich picture of a woman experiencing all of

---

66   Song of Solomon 2:6-7
67   Song of Solomon 4:11-12
68   Song of Solomon 4:12
69   Song of Solomon 4:16

the thrills and the passions of sex, but it requires an understanding man for her to experience all that is her inheritance as a woman.

An understanding man enhances her life

To live in the blessing of a sexually fulfilling marriage requires work. Sometimes, my friend, it requires a lot of work! And guess who should be taking responsibility for that work? All too often, men want to leave that work to the woman. But the Bible says this,

> Husbands, in the same way be considerate as you live with your wives, and treat them with respect as the weaker partner and as heirs with you of the gracious gift of life, so that nothing will hinder your prayers.[70]

You are called to be an ox, not a bull in a china shop. Be a lion on behalf of your wife; learn to guard her heart and to keep her safe. Headship, my friend, is about leadership. When the Bible says that the husband is the head of the wife, it's not about being the boss, it's about accepting a key responsibility for her blessing in life. A man is the head of his wife, and good sex begins with an understanding man. An understanding man knows that the marriage won't experience wonderful, joy-filled, healing sex without teamwork, and the *valiant man* embraces the fact that it begins with him.

As the man, you get to die first. Because of the pressure of male sexuality, sometimes it will *feel* like you are going to die! The fact is that you won't die. If you're willing to learn how to be an understanding man, a man who really knows the way a woman is made and how best to minister to her, serve her and bless her, my friend, you could live the life that other people only dream of. To

---

70   1 Peter 3:7

be married to a happy woman is a blessing beyond description. The tragedy is that all too often a man has no idea how to get there; he does not know how to make her happy.

Sometimes the tragedy is that a man does not know how to undo the tension and the hurt that he feels within his wife. You may feel a lot of resistance in your sex life at home. Well, I have news for you: It's there for a reason. You will need to learn how that resistance began. You will need to learn how to undo some of that damage, because your wife deserves your understanding. Sex was given by God to *make* your marriage, not to *break* your marriage, and I want to work on that with you in this chapter.

Let me share one woman's experience with you through this quote from a book called *Secrets of Eve*:

> Sex is now the most beautiful thing in my marriage. It wasn't always so. It took my husband and me a long time to work out our incompatibility, but it was worth the wait. I wouldn't ever want to be without this wonderful gift from God. Sex does more to bring our marriage together than almost anything else.[71]

This is true for Helen and me as well, but it hasn't always been that way and it hasn't been without a lot of work. If you were to refer to earlier periods in our marriage and ask me to rate out of ten how successful I felt our marriage was, I would have given it a seven. But if you had asked my wife the same question, she may have given it a three. You see, it's very easy for a man to be self-centered. It's easy for a man to be ignorant of the way his wife feels about sex and how she experiences sex from her side of the bedroom. It's so easy for a man to pressure, complain, criticize, belittle, bargain,

---

71   A. Hart, C. Hart Weber, D. Taylor, *Secrets of Eve*, Thomas Nelson Publishers, Nashville, TN, 1994.

threaten, manipulate... and occasionally get what he wants, but he may have to pay a very high price for it. When you invest negativity into your wife's heart you sow into her the feeling that she has to live self-defensively. When you put her under that kind of pressure she comes to learn that her femininity is a burden rather than a blessing. I want to help you undo all that. I want to help you take your marriage and your sexuality to a much better place.

The *valiant man* embraces the call to die first. The *valiant man* is moved by the Ewe Lamb Principle, a concept which I first encountered in Arterburn and Stoeker's book entitled *Every Man's Battle*. The story of King David and Bathsheba is one of the most notorious stories in the Bible—people often know the story even if they've never read the Bible. King David was looking out from the roof of his villa when he saw a neighbor's wife taking a bath on her rooftop. The sight of that naked woman went straight to the sexual arousal chemistry set in David's head, phenylethylamine kicked in, a jolt of euphoria overrode David's better judgment, and he sent for her. And before you could count to ten, he had committed adultery and she was pregnant. To cover the pregnancy, David sent orders to the battle field for her husband, Uriah, to return home, thinking he would sleep with his wife and no one would know whose child it was. But Uriah's loyalty to David and the men he was responsible for on the battlefield precluded sexual intimacy with his wife, so David repaid his profound loyalty by effectively having him murdered in battle.

You would think this story shows David to be a man without morals. Not so. David had morals, but the chemistry set in his own brain had been allowed ascendancy and he became temporarily insane. Sexual arousal has the tendency in men to clamor with an urgency that suppresses higher moral values—unless a man is trained how to respond and control himself honorably. God knew the moral values were there in David, but in that particular circumstance they were submerged under a tidal wave of sexual arousal.

God sent Nathan the prophet with a story about a rich man with lots of cattle. You see, that's how David had treated Bathsheba; as if she was a cow with big udders, made for no other reason than for his pleasure. In Nathan's story, a guest had come to this rich man's house, and wanting to serve up a meal for his guest, he had decided not to kill one of his own cows. Next door, there was a man with a little ewe lamb—it was tender, vulnerable and gentle; that's how Uriah had seen his wife and that's how he had treated her. So the rich man went next door, took the little ewe lamb, slit its throat, and served it up as a meal for his guest.

That's exactly what David had done with his neighbor's wife. When David heard the story, he was enraged and proclaimed, "The man who did this ought to die!" Well, David, we've got some bad news for you, mate. You are the man! The morals were there in David all right, they just needed to be brought to the surface.

Do you want to be an understanding man? Well, this story is for you. I have a photo of my wife beside me on the desk as I write these words, and I'll show you that picture later in the book. It's a picture of my wife at the age of two. She's sitting on a little rocking horse. She's vulnerable and precious. That picture of my wife provokes in me the most profound sense of responsibility. I am an ox, I am a lion, I am an eagle, and I am a man dedicated to her wellbeing. For this little one, I will lay down my life. For this precious being, I have been called to die first. The Ewe Lamb Principle is a core idea in the mind and heart of the understanding man. We've mentioned it before and we will revisit this principle again later in the book. It goes to the core of being a *valiant man*.

God sees the precious innocence of your wife's tender heart and He wants you to guard it, protect it, defend it and build up the emotional security of your wife. God believes that your wife is worth suffering for. An understanding man is willing to make his wife a lifetime study. That's the way to maximize joy for both of you.

Differences between male and female sexuality

You and I need to understand some of the differences between male and female sexuality to see if we can do something about improving the quality of our understanding hearts. As you know from experience, male sexuality is quite simple. For instance, a man tends to live at a fairly constant level of sexual desire. A woman doesn't live in that space, and it's not because she doesn't enjoy sex. She *does* enjoy sex, but it takes more time and the right circumstances for her to get there. Female sexuality is far more complex and affected by more factors than male sexuality. As a result, sex for her is a less relentless and a more variable stream in her life.

As we've already discussed, a primary difference between male and female sexuality is the hormonal engine. Her hormones are very different to yours, and they affect her desire for sex in a way that is very different to yours. As a male, your primary hormonal engine is testosterone. Testosterone levels only marginally rise and fall in a man, although there is a tendency for testosterone levels to fall as a man ages. A woman lives with two other hormones that play a significant role in her life—estrogen and progesterone, and these rise and fall dramatically over the period of a month.

Have you ever asked your wife to explain to you how she feels during that premenstrual period in her life? You see, during this time one hormone has plummeted while the other has risen, and with that come feelings of tension. It affects different women to different degrees; for some women the impact is mild, but for others PMS creates painful emotional tension. In fact, in the United States PMS has been accepted in some cases as a sufficient defense for murder. (I've often reminded my wife that we live in Australia!)

Have you ever wondered what PMS stands for? I used to think it stood for Pre-Menstrual Syndrome, but I've been told by some men that it stands for Punish My Spouse, Permissible Manslaughter or Phenomenal Mood Swings.

Quoting again from the research done on women's sexuality[72], 40% of women say their hormonal cycle, the rising and falling levels of estrogen and progesterone have a significant impact on their desire for sexual intimacy. The same is true of the menstrual cycle. A man has never had to experience a menstrual cycle. A woman has this as part of her regular experience of life. The understanding man makes his wife a lifetime study. How *does* PMS impact your wife? What does the cycle mean in *her* experience? You won't find the answer to these questions in a book—any book. Instead, you'll need to talk to her and listen intently to what she sees. She can help you become an understanding man.

Another issue that can significantly affect a woman's desire for sex is the perception she has of her desirability. Men and women are so different in this respect. Factors that a man would not identify with can have a profound effect on how a woman feels about sex. One factor that really impacts a woman is her weight. Could you in your wildest dreams imagine a man saying to his wife, "Ooh, sweetheart, I couldn't have sex tonight—I feel too fat!"? That's not something that seems to impact a man's thought life, but for a woman it can be a big issue.

Then there is a significant difference in terms of *how often* men and women *think* about sex and the strength of their sexual desire. Research

---

72   *ibid.*

demonstrates that by far the highest proportion of men think about sex daily and many would have to say sex gets into their thoughts hourly. Research indicates that women live in a different space. The highest proportions of women do not think about sex every hour, or even every day. While the pre-occupation with sex for a woman will depend in part on which part of her monthly cycle she is in, the general response of the majority of women is that they would think about sex weekly. In terms of the strength of sexual desire, the highest proportion of men describes their sexual desire as strong, whereas the highest proportion of women describe their sexual desire as moderate.

It's important to recognize that if women talk about sex on a more regular basis, their desire for it tends to increase. It's one of the impacts of the *Sex in the City* syndrome that is touching Western civilization today. If you sexualize a woman's environment, and you continually talk about sex, her thinking about sex tends to raise her desire for sex. It would be the same for you and your wife. The way you share and converse with one another about sexual intimacy is important. Tragically, if the only time you and your wife ever talk about intimacy, relationship and sex is when you want to have some, then your wife would tend not to engage in that conversation; the only time it's discussed is when she is under pressure. That means she won't grow in her desire for sexual intimacy. The way you converse with your wife about intimacy and the degree to which you share your hearts with one another on a daily basis will have a direct impact on the quality of your sex life.

We need to recognize that a woman's sexual desires are affected profoundly by her daily environment and her circumstances. For instance, how many children does she have? How busy is her life at the moment? Are the children on holiday and therefore home all day? For a mum with two or three school-age children, holidays are a nightmare because she rarely has a break from morning until night. You have got to understand that such a situation will rob her of much of her desire for sexual intimacy.

Finding the energy for sex

Research indicates that nearly 50%of married women say that one of the biggest challenges they face with sexual intimacy is simply finding the energy for it. Now, 30% say that one of the difficulties is actually feeling the desire for it. Reaching orgasm is a difficulty for 25% of women. Becoming aroused is a challenge for 20% of women. The most interesting factor in this research is that the largest issue regarding sexual intimacy for a married woman is simply that she can't find the energy.

Research demonstrates that a lot of that has to do with age and the season of life in which a woman finds herself. It's not difficult to figure out why it might be that between the ages of about 30 to 45 women experience the greatest difficulty in finding energy for sex. This is the age where most women are raising children and many are working outside the home as well. As women grow older and home life becomes less stressful and less demanding, the energy for sex increases so that often the increased joy in the pleasure of sex comes at a later age.

Now, as a man you can do something about that. Have you ever talked to your wife about how you could try to help her find more energy for sex? Sexual intimacy with your wife could improve if you take on more responsibilities around the home. By the way, this is another example of benign self-interest. You want to serve her partly because she is worth it, but as a by-product she just might find the energy for something that would be a delight to you and a blessing to your relationship. It's a real issue for a woman raising children to find energy for intimacy. For instance, 55% of women with children at home said finding energy for sex was a real challenge for them. The issue of children at home adds greatly to the wear and tear on a woman's life; so obviously you must either help her or be considerate about that fact and not expect her to be constantly available and energetic about sexual intimacy.

As I said earlier, one of the differences between male and female sexuality concerns body image. Research suggests that about 40% of women say their body image affects sexual desire, and almost 30% of women say their weight affects their desire for sexual intimacy. Other important factors in descending order of importance to women are how fit they feel, menopause, and tiredness and stress. It really does matter to a woman if she doesn't feel very sexy or attractive. It makes a great deal of difference when a man continually assures his wife that she is attractive to him, that he thinks she's wonderful. You cannot overdo your ministry to your wife, especially if it helps her deal with the stress of her own body image. While body image is a common issue for women, most men don't identify much with this at all. So it's important that you help her resolve her concerns about body weight and body image.

Another difference is that female sexual desire diminishes during childbearing, but male sexual desire does not. If a woman is pregnant, her level of sexual desire drops off considerably. You and I need to recognize that because a male doesn't experience that same low point, we need to be extra careful to understand the challenge a woman faces during their childbearing experience. Remember, you are the head of your wife, and that means you get to die first.

The *valiant man* must also be mindful that female sexuality is far more easily damaged by trauma and abuse. Women are subjected to more trauma and abuse than men. More women are the target of inappropriate sexual behavior from men than the other way around. It traumatizes them and damages them much more profoundly than we might imagine. Careforce Lifekeys has created the Door of Hope program to bring healing to women who are survivors of sexual abuse. If your wife is one of the many women whose life experience includes the painful reality of abuse, encourage her to take the opportunity to restore her own soul. It requires an understanding man to help his wife come through an experience of abuse or trauma. And you, my friend, as a caring and understanding man, are a part of the answer to that problem.

Sex and the influence of adrenaline

Whilst male sexuality easily gets linked with adrenalin excitement, this is not true for women… and significant conflict can result! When a man finds himself linking his sex drive with adrenalin, it manifests itself in a number of disturbing ways for a woman. A man, for example, can become rougher and adopt crude speech. However, often that is such a turn-off for women. He gets all excited, his adrenalin is pumping away, and his sex drive is on high alert, but out of his mouth comes an aggressive and highly sexualized language that sounds abusive and dirty to a woman. That is simply not helpful.

A man under the influence of increased adrenalin and excitement can want to press a woman to do things sexually that would be very exciting to him but may be offensive, painful or embarrassing to her. As a man, you need to appreciate that what may be very exciting and highly charged for you could be abusive and harmful for her. You see, she does not experience what you experience. That's not the way her system is wired, so you will need to guard yourself under those circumstances. Guard and protect your Ewe Lamb. Don't ever wound her or damage her in your search for sexual delight.

A key difference between men and women is the fact that sexual arousal for men is easily triggered by the visual. Men only have to see a bit of underwear and the excitement level rises. But a woman gets excited when a man gets relational. It's all too easy for a man to live disconnected emotionally from his wife, with little communication and little tenderness all day long. You have to deal with the fact that you might be a microwave, but she's a crock pot. You want something tender from her at 9 o'clock tonight? Well, you needed to turn her on at 9 o'clock this morning. She needed you to leave home in the morning with a soft touch of the hand, a tender kiss, a warm hug, and some kind words. She would have loved a phone call from you during the day to see how she was going. Instead, she's heard nothing from you all day. She would have loved you to come home and wrap your arms around her and just hold her close, listen to her day, rub her shoulders and tell her she is the most important thing in your life.

You could have stimulated some of those touch receptors and given her a dose of oxytocin which would have made her feel loved and cared for. But you came home cranky, sat in a chair, and watched television. There's been no expression of tenderness between you. Then at 9 o'clock that night you've seen some underwear and *bam!* You suddenly think it ought to be happening right now! You have no idea! You're suddenly excited, but she's not receptive to romantic advances right now. She's still hurting from your cranky words and wondering if she matters to anyone. You've got a lot of work to do before you can expect what you're hoping for.

It's the understanding man who has the joy of feeling her respond to his touch, because it's the understanding man who has turned her on in the morning and now she's ready to respond. Remember, she's turned on by relationship. An understanding man is very wary of his own tendency to suddenly be excited and ready for sex when he knows his wife has had no opportunity to be stimulated to the same degree because he has not given her the attention she needs to be capable of the tender responsiveness he longs for.

What women like most and least about sex

Do you want to know what married women say they like most about sex? Research reveals that above all, they like both the physical closeness and the emotional closeness; they want to *feel* close. Women also enjoy the *time* spent together with their husbands. It's not that physical release is unimportant; an orgasm is important to a woman, but it is not her highest priority. For a man, it is the highest priority. It's not that women don't enjoy orgasm; it's just not as highly prioritized for them.

What do women like least about sex? Women just don't like the mess. So, you need to be prepared. The thoughtful man will ensure that he brings towels (or whatever it takes) to the bed so that this negative effect is minimized. Women are made of sugar and spice and all things nice. Men are made of slugs and snails and puppy dogs' tails. Men couldn't care less about mess. Our response to mess is: *Who cares? As long as we're having fun!* But for a woman it matters, so you need to do what you can to help.

The understanding man wants to give his wife the best possible experience. He wants to make sure she enjoys the intimacy of sex. So he is always careful to ensure her needs are met. A man's smell can be very attractive to a woman, but there comes a point at which a shower would really do him a whole lot of good. So would the investment in a decent aftershave or cologne. He needs to ensure that he is providing for his wife an experience of joy, not something she has to tolerate or endure. It's not uncommon for men to place a lower priority on grooming. For the average woman, grooming matters—so groom! That means you shave, shower, clean your teeth, splash on cologne (find out what she likes)... And take care of the surroundings. The more care you show, the more it signals the value you place on her experience of intimacy—and it counts!

Research shows that women love a husband's affirmation. Your words count. The understanding man lets this reality sink in. It matters to the woman you love that you use words that are not crude, that are not humiliating, that don't cause the experience to degenerate into something that they feel is animalistic. A thoughtful man will take that into consideration.

For both men and for women, the brain remains the primary organ that controls sex. So think tender, caring thoughts. And speak tender, caring words. Read passages from the Song of Solomon—the writer uses a fountain of expressive words to extol the beauty of his beloved and the delight felt in the encounter. Crank up your vocal tenderness—learn some poetry if you can't think of your own words. Create a thought life and an environment in which the communication is warm, connected, relational and safe.

I know this won't come as a surprise to you, but research shows there is a strong association between marital happiness and sexual satisfaction. It's rare to find an unhappy marriage in which the husband and wife experience good sex. Sexual satisfaction plays a huge role in a good marriage. For this reason, it really is worth an investment both in your time and in your energy. Good sex is not only a product of a great marriage it is one of the causes.

Develop closeness with your woman

Every man at some point wants to develop a close relationship with the woman he loves. However, many of us don't know how to do that. Men are not always as relationally competent as the woman they love, so closeness with a woman doesn't always come easily. Here are some ideas to help you in that area:

+ Focus on your partner's positive qualities.
+ Spend more time together.

+ Really listen to your partner.
+ Say "I love you!" often.
+ Compliment, affirm and praise your partner.

These tips are very obvious, and yet every one of us can *know* something but fail to put it into practice. If you were to act on every one of these five tips over the next week, you would see a dramatic improvement in your relationship with your loved one. Remember, when you focus on your partner's weaknesses, you destroy her and cause her to want to hide from you. Focus on her positive qualities instead, and you will see her respond positively. Overall, spend time with her and really listen to what she is saying. Constantly say to her, "I love you! I love you! I love you!" You can never tell a woman too many times that you love her. Compliment her, affirm her, praise her and build her up. These are some of the great keys to developing a good sexual relationship.

Increase your energy levels

Now, do you want to learn how to increase your wife's energy levels? Women's lives are so busy these days, especially if they are raising children. Often sexual intimacy goes out the window because you are both exhausted at the end of the day. So you both need to learn how to keep your energy levels up if you want to enhance intimacy with each other. Here are some of my tips:

+ **Simplify your life.** Get rid of the clutter and busyness that builds up around marriage and family life. If you really want to improve sexual intimacy with your wife, then make the necessary sacrifices to simplify and de-clutter your days.

+ **Sleep more.** Turn off the television, stop any work you may be doing at home, and deliberately go to bed earlier so that before you both pass out on the bed you can enjoy more time together for communication—not just for sexual intimacy, but to simply be together and share life together.

+ **Share household chores and daily family life.** Be the ox in your family and carry the burden for your wife in ways that allow her to sit, relax and feel cared for.

+ **Move your body!** I think it is really great for married couples to regularly exercise. Develop a pattern for your exercise. Schedule a certain number of days in the week to get up early and take your wife for a walk. Or mind the children while she gets active. The fitter she is, the less stressed she will be and the more she'll feel like sexual intimacy.

+ **Laugh.** Laughter has amazing powers to release the soul. Have a happy home. The more you laugh, the better your sex life will be.

What basic tips these are! However, one of the reasons for declining sexual interest in marriages is that you are both so tired. The result is that the only occasions when sexual intimacy takes place in your home are when both your energy levels are simply too low to make sex what it really could be.

Tackle body image distortions

As I've said before, body image is a huge issue for a woman. So you will need to affirm and reassure your wife persistently. You cannot tell her too frequently that you think she is wonderful, that you think she is beautiful, that she touches your heart. Help her to accept herself. Women wrestle with questions like: "Am I still beautiful? Does he still think I'm pretty?" So consistently compliment her inner beauty. Help your wife to appreciate that she is more than a body. Help her to realize over and over again that you think she is a wonderful human being and that you love her— not just because she is a woman, but because she is an amazing person.

You can also tackle body image distortions by addressing health issues. And I'm not just talking about *her* health. You may need to improve your own body image, like working on your fitness, grooming and personal hygiene, and losing excess weight. Keep yourself as fit as possible so that you can make your sexual intimacy last all the days of your life.

Variety in lovemaking

It always helps to have some variety in your lovemaking. Sex does not need to be mundane and run-of-the-mill. The danger in saying this to a man is that he assumes this means coming up with some new position, wrapping himself in glad wrap, or doing something weird or mildly perverted. For a woman, it matters that you put some thought into the relationship, and that your sex life is not a matter of simply declaring, "It's Tuesday night, so let's do it!"

Sometimes what a marriage needs is some **fast food sex**. This is sex when one or both of you are busy. Fast food sex is the ability to simply enjoy each other and laugh and experience sex in the little time you have. But don't presume that because she honored you with a spontaneous burst of pleasure that from now on you can make that the staple diet of your sex life!

Then there is the standard **meat and potato sex**. One of the great advantages of sexual intimacy between a man and his wife—where a great relationship of care and trust exists—is the fact that sexual intimacy isn't about novelty. Instead, it's about allowing sex to be what it is—the intimacy that heals and knits and affirms your relationship.

Then there's **gourmet sex**. Here I am referring to those times when you book a hotel room and take her away. You let her dress up, you take her out, treat her like royalty and make sexual intimacy a special occasion. It may cost a bit more money, but she is worth the investment! It's all about her. You take her shopping, let her browse as much as she wants, dote on her, and enjoy the response as she delights in being a delight.

Hints for sexual enhancement

It is a simple but vital fact that women are far more sensitive to their environment than men. For a man, the room doesn't have to be particularly secure. He's not particularly self-conscious about where sexual intimacy takes place, but that's not the case for a woman. You may find it helpful to secure a lock on the door, and get a phone with a ringer switch so that loud phone calls don't interrupt you. There is nothing more jarring for a woman involved in sexual intimacy than suddenly feeling a shock of fear when she thinks somebody may be approaching the room, or the phone rings and frightens the daylights out of her. These interruptions put a shot of adrenalin through her system that takes her from relaxation to tension, and it is hard work for her to relax again. This does not enhance sexual intimacy. Orgasm is a relaxation response and it is not possible to be tense and relax at the same time.

As I mentioned earlier, another tip is intentional early bedtimes. It's really helpful to get into bed before you are both totally worn out. Then you'll find some wonderful additional time together in the evenings. But don't make this time just about sex. Make sure you practice non-sexual touching, because one of the things that make a woman nervous is that the only time her man touches her is when he wants sex. One of the ways to defuse that is to learn to touch your wife non-sexually. Massage her shoulders, rub her feet, and hold hands while you talk. Learn to care for her without any sexual expectations whatsoever. This goes a long way towards helping her learn that you want to touch her because you care about her, not because you expect something immediately in return.

Make it your goal to cultivate your wife's success in sexual intimacy. I wish I had learned earlier in our marriage about the clitoris. I wish I had learned earlier about how to help my wife experience orgasm. We were married for about ten years before I read the book by Tim and Beverly LaHaye, *The Act of Marriage*.[73] It was through reading that book that I discovered some things my parents never told me… in fact, nobody had ever told me. Reading that book together with my wife helped me begin to cultivate success for her. When you help your wife to successfully and beautifully experience sexual intimacy, you build her confidence in herself. Research reveals that as a woman gets older her desire for sex tends to increase. Over time she can build greater confidence in the fact that sexual intimacy with her husband will be both a thrilling and a successful experience. You can cultivate that in your wife by learning how to help her and care for her in sexual intimacy.

If you're unsure about how to help your wife achieve orgasm, then you need to find out more. Her experience of sex will be dependent on your willingness to learn and become the under-

---

73   T. & B. LaHaye, *The Act of Marriage*, Zondervan Publishing, Grand Rapids, MI, 1998.

standing man she needs you to be. Read books. Talk to her and tell her you want to learn… that it's not about *your* feelings, but it's about *hers*. Realize that she has probably not been taught to be aware of the function of her body. She has likely grown up with the 'don't touch' rule. Help her—and yourself—find out about your mutual physiology. Tell her that no truth she needs to tell you about your approach will be too unpleasant to hear if it will help you to be the man she needs you to be. Don't let your pride or your hurt feelings stop you from learning whatever you need to learn to give your wife the success she was born for.

Rest assured in the knowledge that the many differences between you and your wife are God-given. Don't expect your wife to adopt your unique male sexuality as the norm. You are testosterone-driven, she isn't. You are a man, she isn't. Allow her to be what she is, and allow her femininity to blossom. That means recognizing and fitting into her patterns of rising and falling sexual desires. Allow her to be who she is: beautifully unique and a complement to you. Don't try to turn her into you. Simply love her for who she is, and over time lead her into an increasing confidence that you can be trusted with her sexuality, because you will guard it and keep it; you will never ravage it, you will never plunder it, and you won't be a taker at her expense. Lay down your life for your ewe lamb.

Singles and sex

"But what about singles?" I hear you ask. One respondent in an extensive survey conducted by Dr. Archibald Hart said this:

"Since you can only give it once, I decided at an early age to give 'the gift' only to the man who would love me for the rest of my life. I was blessed to marry a man with the same goal, and now coming up on our one-year anniversary we cherish this gift. I am saddened, even angered, by the lies society tells about pre-marital sex. It is stealing a beautiful experience from so many young people. Waiting was the best choice I ever made!"[74]

Every young man who is yet to be married needs to know that a young woman wants to be loved by a man who is willing to sacrifice his own agenda for her protection. One of the greatest gifts a young man can give to the woman he is courting is self-control. That means giving a woman the privilege of not having to continually guard the gates of purity. A *valiant man*, even though his hormones are pressing him to take what he wants, guards his behavior, protects his ewe lamb keeps her safe. A *valiant man* does not put any woman under pressure; he guards her dignity and her purity. Be that man!

It is very damaging for a woman to have to constantly resist unhelpful pressure to have sexual intercourse or engage in sexual activity. A young *valiant man* who is growing in his purity will not prey on the woman he loves. Instead, he will guard her and protect her. I created a course for young singles called The Search for Intimacy[75]. If you need some discipleship as a young single, I commend it to you. Be a *valiant man*, and be an *understanding man*.

---

74   The Hart Report, taken from *Secrets of Eve* by Archibald D. Hart, Catherine Hart Weber and Debra Taylor.

75   Visit www.careforcelifekeys.org and follow the links to The Search for Intimacy

REFLECTION

Women and men are different, but these differences can be transcended through understanding, through acceptance and through persistence. My friend, if you become an understanding man. You will have a happier wife, and this I believe is not only the will of God for you, it is the will of God for her. So make it your business from this day onwards to do whatever you can to become an understanding man, for you will be richly rewarded.

Begin today. Take some of the ideas I have outlined in this chapter, and put them into practice.

CHAPTER 7

RETRAINING YOUR BRAIN

"Good habits result from resisting temptation."
Ancient Proverb

"A sound mind in a sound body is a short but full description
of a happy state in this world."
John Locke

God takes your personal purity seriously. After all, it's His idea. I've been speaking to people of all ages on the subject of sexual purity for many years now, so I know from experience that the quest for personal purity is a war zone, and our Creator expects us to fight. Victory in this battle demands the exercise of your will, but not perhaps in the way you might expect. The exercise of your will is not primarily about trying really hard *not* to do unhelpful things again. Instead, it's primarily about being determined to do the work necessary to retrain your brain.

So why do you need to retrain your brain? And what's wrong with your brain in the first place? Well, the three biggest challenges most men need to bring under control are fantasy, pornography and masturbation. Fantasy is imaginary sex and it includes the way a man thinks about sex. Pornography is the use of images of one kind or another to excite and manipulate sexual arousal. The third challenge many men contend with is masturbation; self-induced orgasm or lonely sex. All three of these challenges have the potential to be destructive forces in our lives.

However, not all fantasy is destructive. You see, God designed us to be creative beings. He gave us a mind, an imagination and an anticipation, all of which are a part of the joy of intimate relationships. But some aspects of fantasy are not appropriate. Some of it has the potential to be very destructive, which is why we need to know how to handle it.

Human sexual behavior is largely learned behavior, which means that it can also be unlearned. However, in order to unlearn negative, destructive behavior, we need to engage the brain. The brain is an amazing organ; it is the hardware of human personality. When you damage the brain, you damage human personality. Likewise, when you mould the brain, you mould human personality. Your brain is similar to a computer in some ways. A computer is the hardware for the programs you run on it, so if you damage the computer then the programs simply won't run in the same way. But, unlike a computer, your brain has the ability to change and adapt to challenges and threats. And it changes depending on how you use it. You and I can—and should—learn how to make the most out of this amazing equipment we've been given. So let's get started...

Love maps in your brain

While your brain processes conscious thought at about 250 words a minute, it *processes* stimuli and reactions at a rate of about 1250 words a minute. That's what makes speed reading possible and allows for accurate split second reactions behind the wheel of a car. It's both a helpful and unhelpful feature of the brain's capacity.

Your brain operates electrochemically. It receives and processes sensory information from all over the body at electric speed, and most of it happens subconsciously. In other words, most of the processing in the brain is done without conscious awareness. We tend not to be aware of this until a situation produces a reaction which gets our attention. For example, you can walk through an office full of women without any noticeable impact, but suddenly—without warning—one person in that room full of people grabs your attention and your head turns in that direction without you making a conscious decision to do so. You may need to make a conscious decision to turn away again, and that's what bouncing the eyes is about.

Inside every one of us is a "love map". We're not sure how that love map is created, but we do know that certain stimuli trigger that love map inside us. We may see a face, smell some perfume or hear a voice, and our brain processes all the information at a speed beyond our ability to anticipate it. Our first awareness that something has happened are the physiological signs of arousal; our love map has been triggered and snaps us to attention.

I experienced this situation as a young school teacher in 1972. As I mentioned in a previous chapter, I was boarding a bus to take a group of students on a trip across to Tasmania. I have no idea why, but on that bus one face suddenly stood out. I remember the girl was wearing a beret and she was dressed up ready for the trip. When my eyes saw her face, there was an instantaneous reaction. I simply became aware that something had been triggered inside me with explosive force.

Those who study this phenomenon have framed the term "love map" to describe the experience. It's as if there are a series of stimuli that are wired into a person's personality, so that when you come across certain situations, those stimuli that fit your love map alert your brain to fixate your attention on the object, sound, feel or smell before you. It can be a combination of many factors: the sound of a voice, the shape of a body, the shape of a face or the smell of a certain perfume. When enough of those stimuli fit your love map, you are impacted in such a way that the moment can take your breath away! You become aware that something just happened to you that caused your body and your brain to react, yet you may not be able to explain rationally how or why.

Neurochemical patterns in your brain

Those of us who drive have all had a parallel experience behind the wheel of a car. When you're driving a car, especially over a route you have traveled many times before, you can drive from one place to another without being conscious of what you are doing. During the car journey, your mind is active, your ears are hearing, your eyes are seeing, and your body is sensing vibrations from the road. All of that is going through your brain at a speed of 1250 words a minute, but you can arrive at your destination without remembering the specific details of the journey, even though it may have occurred very recently and over a short time span. Your brain has been processing information at electric speed, and yet most of the time it didn't trigger your conscious awareness.

Driving along a well known route your reactions are often unconscious. Suddenly something approaches your path that catches your attention. You might see a blur of movement out of your peripheral vision and instantly your foot punches the brake—not because you thought about the situation and made a conscious decision, but because your brain processes all the information about five times faster than you can consciously assess the situation. That blur of movement out of the corner of your vision triggers a reaction out of the brain tracks you've formed over years of driving experience. That special ability of the brain can help save your life, and it might help save the life of a dog or cat that bolted from the roadside into your path. Without thinking, there is enough in that stimulus to trigger a reaction in your brain, so that you hit the brake, pull the car to the left, and miss killing that wayward animal. Once the danger is averted, your heart beats fast and you think: *Whoa! Lucky little pooch!*

Your brain's amazing capacity to react with speed on the basis of brain tracks learned over a period of time can be both helpful and unhelpful. It can be of great benefit to you when a dog runs into the path of your speeding car. But it's not that helpful when a beautiful woman crosses the footpath in front of you. The same brain behavior that triggers a reaction with your braking foot will also follow the brain tracks laid down over years of sexual arousal from the sight of pretty women. Your sexuality is fired up at the same speed as your driving reactions. So before you consciously think of it, your brain reacts to the stimulus of the woman with amazing speed. Your brain simply follows familiar grooves and pathways much faster than you can consciously keep up. Your brain has the ability to run ahead of your conscious thoughts at lightening speed.

It's important you understand that your brain works in that way. Otherwise you'll assume at some point that you are morally defective, or perhaps demon possessed, because your sexual arousal mechanisms continue to react to the impact of women long after you've made the decision that you want to be a *valiant man*. Don't beat yourself up over those emotional reactions that happen so quickly and intrusively when it comes to sex. Beating yourself up will not help. What *will* help is learning how the control patterns in your brain are established and triggered. Learn the skills to set your life on a long-term path of restoration.

Mental tracks through your brain

Now here's some more information about your amazing brain. Every brain cell has an incredible capacity to store information. Brain cells do not touch each other; they transmit information from one to another across a gap (synapse) via neurotransmitters swimming through a chemical jelly called acetylcholine. Every cell in your brain is living in that jelly, and in order for one cell to communicate with another it must transmit its message across the synapse through that jelly.

Passing messages through acetylcholine down a chain of brain cells results in the formation of a "pathway"—a bit like a cattle track across a field—virtually creating mental tracks in your brain. Once a pathway has been established information runs down that track without you having to think a great deal. Most of your life is spent living out of those tracks which you have either deliberately or inadvertently created by allowing a stimulus to be processed down certain pathway to produce a reaction of some kind. Driving a car would be an emotional nightmare if we did not have the capacity to create these tracks and then allow them to do a lot of the processing while we focus on the one or two things that *do* demand more focus.

You may have heard of the term *muscle memory*. If you're a keen golfer like I am, you will know that one of the ways to improve your game is to try to create muscle memory in your brain. Muscle memory is created by hitting the ball constantly with the same swing pattern so that your brain fires your muscles automatically and produces the same result every time. Well, that's the challenge of golf, isn't it! We're always trying to hit a small white ball the same way every time. If you practice enough, then every time you line up a shot your brain will mysteriously work out the distance to the hole, how hard to hit the ball, how to grip the club, the sequence in which different muscles must be fired, and so on. As a result, hitting the ball is not a matter of conscious thought. It is a reliance on the capacity of your brain to fire signals to all the different muscles at just the right instant—firing them down the pre-programmed track you've spent so much time creating on the practice fairway… and much faster than you can describe or consciously think about. Executed as planned this produces a shot that makes you glad you're alive. If you're really good at it, you will make a lot of money. If you're not good at it, you will lose golf balls all the time, because the trees and the traps are never in the right places!

Your muscle memory helps you pre-program your golf swing over a period of time. In the same way, the jelly called acetylcholine locks in pathways for your thoughts, and those pathways automatically begin to determine your reactions to certain stimuli. Those pathways in your brain establish a habitual reaction when certain stimuli register in your brain. As has been described already, these tracks work both for good and for evil. They can help you avoid hitting a dog on the road or they can trigger a strong sexual reaction when a beautiful woman comes into view.

Brain tracks can be triggered by stimuli of which you are not conscious. For example, you can find yourself having a sudden impulse to turn on the television to look for a sexually explicit program. Why? Well, something inside your brain has been triggered and run down a familiar pathway, causing a desire or a longing to surface in your emotions which is now influencing your decision making. Up to this point, you haven't made a conscious decision. You may stop to wonder. *Why did that happen? Why am I suddenly feeling this urge?* It isn't always possible to answer that question. It helps when you can.

You see, acetylcholine locks in pathways either for good or for evil, and once they form a track in your brain, your thoughts will head in that direction faster than you can consciously think about it. This is a learned pattern. When the first link in that chain reaction is stimulated, signals travel down that chain right to the end before you become consciously aware of those thoughts.

The bad news is that once that chain has been set in place, you cannot remove the links along that chain. You can never remove a chain once it has been established. This is part of a man's struggle with his sexuality. Since the moment you were born, you have been experiencing stimuli that began to develop pathways of responses to your sexuality. When they have been acted on and thought about over a period of time, they become established pathways. Once a chain has been established, it will be with you for life. You cannot eradicate it. You will feel the impulses and the tensions of that pathway off and on for the rest of your life—both positively and negatively.

Gifted communicator and international teacher, Sy Rogers, has spoken publicly of his experience of this dynamic in his own life. He became a Christian as he was preparing to undergo a sex-change operation. He had come to the conclusion that he was a failure as a man, so he might as well try life as a woman. He had been involved in the gay lifestyle for many years. There had been tracks of emotional responses to stimuli leading to homosexual behavior that had been grafted into his mind. When I spoke to him about his experience of life as a Christian he had been walking with Christ for 25 years. He acknowledged that 25 years later a stimulus can still provoke an old brain track to echo an old feeling or a past longing in his life. The strength of an old track may fade with time, but old echoes from the past can still emerge at unexpected times and in unexpected places.

Creating new tracks in your brain

The good news is that whilst those tracks cannot be eradicated, you can learn to divert your thinking around them and create new tracks. A habitual chain can't be undone, but it can be replaced; you *can* retrain your brain for new responses.

Every man must accept responsibility to steward his body, his mind, and his sex drive. God will not take your sexuality or your sex drive away. Instead, He calls you to a life of discipleship and obedience. Every man must accept responsibility for his thoughts, his behaviors, and for the renewing of his mind. This is a challenge for all men, and especially for men who have a religious or spiritual element in their lives.

If we don't understand the hardware of our brain and how it

works, we can find ourselves praying frustrating and pointless prayers. "God, take these feelings away from me!" you may plead. But you need to realize that whilst you can pray that prayer for a decade, it is likely not to be answered. If you have been praying along those lines, what you have been saying to God is this: "Lord, for years I have allowed bad thoughts to form unholy tracks in my mind. Would you take those tracks away?" But God does not take those tracks away. Instead, He asks you to rebuild your brain with new ones. If you don't understand that, you can find yourself pleading with God for something that He isn't going to do for you, and that will be very frustrating for you.

The Bible says, "Hope deferred makes the heart sick."[76] Praying for something that never comes almost certainly leads to a false conclusion: *Maybe God doesn't love me or care about me.* It's not that God doesn't love you, nor is it the case that He won't hear your cry or your prayer. The fact is that you don't understand how this process works. You wouldn't do that with your driving, would you? For instance, you wouldn't say to God, "God, I react the wrong way when my car starts skidding on a wet and slippery road, so please take my wrong reaction away from me." No, you would take responsibility for your driving and declare, *My normal reaction when people and animals cross my path on wet roads is to jam my foot on the brake and that's not safe for me or my passengers, so I had better take a course in safe driving and learn how to react better when driving on wet roads.*

In the same way, your response to wrong sexual thoughts needs to be, *If my brain tracks result in unhealthy reactions in my life, I need to accept responsibility for the retraining of my brain.* Don't pray for God to take away your libido. It won't happen. Don't pray for

God to change your brain. It's your brain, so accept responsibility for it. Understanding what is required for you to make progress can improve your driving, your golf, and your level of freedom with regards your sexual purity. This process is called *renewing the mind.*

You renew your mind biologically, not just spiritually

Sy Rogers has spent a lifetime proving to the world that sexual struggles don't have to be life-controlling.[77] Men who have no relationship with God have been able to successfully retrain the neurological patterns in their brain, and yet many Bible college graduates and ministers have continued to struggle with pornography, masturbation and unclean fantasy, even as they fervently pray for change. The reason for this is that renewing the mind is as much a *biological* action as it is a *spiritual* action.

Christians need to realize that renewing the mind is not essentially a spiritual act that results from some mystical process that God does inside our head. If you think the renewing of the mind comes as a miracle in answer to a prayer like, "Oh, God, renew my mind. Touch my brain!", then you misunderstand how the machinery works.

The Word of God is essential to your life, but you have got to do what it says for it to make a world of difference in your life. Let me explain it this way: You don't have to love Jesus to learn to drive a car. And you don't learn to drive a car by praying, "Lord, give me the gift of driving." If you are shown how to manage the machinery—the brakes, accelerator and steering wheel—and you're willing to practice doing the right things often enough, then

---

77   Tape 3 of a six-part series by Sy Rogers entitled *Lessons Learned.* Available from www.syrogers.com.

you can successfully learn to drive a car. You don't even have to read the manual to be able to drive. You just have to be consistent with what the manual says.

Driving is an apt analogy for retraining the brain in sexual responses. The more you drive, the more the pathways are established that allow you to do it without consciously thinking about it. Most of us can drive a car and get to where we need to go without ever making a challenging decision. Most of what happens when we drive is simply neuronal pathways responding automatically. Unless there's a crisis, you don't even have to think about what you have to do to get where you want to go. What *is* challenging is trying to do something that you *haven't* established as a pathway, especially when it brings you into conflict with pathways you've already established.

The first time I traveled to the USA I borrowed a friend's car. Now, I had been driving in Australia since the age of 18, which means I had done a lot of driving on the left-hand side of the road. I remember sitting in my friend's Chevy Astro Van in the hotel car park going over in my head how I would drive out into the traffic and successfully navigate the vehicle along the right-hand lane of the North American road system. When I was ready, I drove out of the car park onto the road, stopped at the traffic lights, and suddenly found myself facing five lanes of cars heading in my direction. I panicked, did a u-turn, and drove straight back into the hotel car park and sat there with my heart pounding, thinking: *How did that just happen?* Sadly, three days later I drove my friend's car into the side of another car right in front of Disneyland, simply because I was fighting twenty years of brain tracks established in Australia. All that training in my brain was not helping my driving experience in the USA. In fact, it was now partly my problem, because even though I was thinking furiously about how to drive correctly, much of my training was instinctively sending me down the wrong pathway.

Constructing off-ramps in your brain

The key to the retraining of your brain is the construction of an off-ramp at the point where an unhelpful track commences. In 1997, *TIME Magazine* published an article on this topic and one of the writers stated: "One of the most helpful messages coming out of the current research is that the biochemical abnormalities associated with addiction can be reversed through learning." A man can have an unhealthy track with him for the rest of his life, but the good news is that he can construct an off-ramp that diverts his thoughts down a newly established healthy track. Renewing your mind requires that you learn to obey the call of God to a new direction in life, and that you learn to pursue this new way of responding even when you're under pressure. This is where exercising your will is critical in the process.

A married man may tend to drift off into fantasy sex whenever he faces challenges in his relationship with his wife. He needs to understand that the fantasy life he is living in his head is an enemy of his relationship with his wife. With help he can come to realize the need to develop a new response whenever his feelings are hurt or whenever he begins to feel lonely. With help he can develop an off-ramp and learn a new response to those feelings. While he's implementing that new response and establishing that new brain track he will need to exercise his will especially when pressure comes, because that old pattern will continue to pressure him to respond as he used to. This is where the exercise of your will is essential.

In chapter three I suggested bouncing your eyes away from images that lead you to wrong responses. When you walk into an office and see an attractive girl, the old brain track immediately provokes a desire to continue looking. This is where you need an off-ramp. You need to deliberately intersect that old brain path and form a new one in which every woman you meet is viewed with dignity and respect. It takes determination and persistence to create a new brain track and it begins with the off-ramp. When you make a decision to activate the *valiant man* discipleship process and you begin to turn your eyes away—*that* is an off-ramp. You have to *do* it. If you don't exercise your will and do what you know you must do, you'll not be successful at creating a new track in your brain, and this means you may never win in your battle for sexual purity. Turning away is not enough in itself—it's just the off-ramp. But without an off-ramp (a behavior that breaks the old pattern and pathway), a new pathway will not be formed.

Within a year of practicing this exercise of bouncing my eyes away from certain images, I became a different person. In fact, during that year I went on a beach holiday and had the opportunity to road test the outcome of months of exercising the behavior of averting my eyes. I was able to trial my new brain track. As you may know, when you're standing on a popular beach, everywhere you look there are women dressed in bikinis—and sometimes they're *missing* part of the bikini! Because I had developed the ability to instantaneously go to that off-ramp whenever I become aware that my eyes had seen something that was attractive to my sexuality, I was able to simply turn away immediately. This had become part of my new mental armory. And it worked!

For us men, our fantasy world will be the next big frontier. Fantasies are simply thoughts that have developed a life of their own. To become valiant men, we are going to have to deal with those fantasies and judge them. The first step is to learn the simple, practical skill of turning your head. If you don't learn this you'll never win, but that's just the first step. The second step is to judge your thought patterns. Satan's fall was the product of an un-judged fantasy. We have to realize that un-judged thought processes, once triggered, run their course at 1250 words a minute. It only takes one brief glance to trigger a response, and in a flash a chain reaction of thoughts and possibilities has run all the way down to fantasy sex before you've made a conscious choice to go there.

Now, if you don't judge the thought life that has been triggered in your imagination, you could walk around for the next 20 minutes with unworthy thoughts about sex and girls fixated on imaginary circumstances and situations. Your mind could continue to run in that fantasy sex pattern for minutes or hours unless you break in and judge your thought life. You may have built your off-ramp and you may have turned your head, but now you must *judge* the thoughts and begin to create a new thought life. Retraining the brain requires that you deliberately judge your thought patterns, build an off-ramp, and take your thoughts to godly places.

Remember that the first step is to bounce your eyes away from inappropriate, sexually stimulating sights. Total sexual sobriety is essential. You cannot afford to indulge yourself for a moment. You must learn to starve unhelpful fantasies of their stimulus. In the past, you may have allowed yourself to look, triggered a sexual fantasy of some kind, and let your mind stay in that fantasy world until something else distracted you. But that was the old pattern working in your mind. You have read enough now to know better.

When you face the same scenario again, you'll know to turn your head away, because you now realize the importance of refusing both the look and the mental fantasyland you have been visiting. You are on your way from *good* man to *valiant* man. Give no place to the things which have stimulated that fantasy world in the past, so let's just say it once more: remove *all* pornography in all its forms from your life. Don't leave a thing. Pornography is food for unclean fantasies. You must starve those unhelpful fantasies if you are serious about winning the battle for sexual purity.

Disrupting the ANTS in your life

In the process of building off-ramps and retraining your brain, you are learning a new skill—the skill of disrupting unhealthy thought patterns. Building an off-ramp begins by interrupting the old pattern. Get the *ANTs out of your pants!* Confront them!

Let's just imagine you're walking down the street and an attractive woman catches your eye, triggering an Automatic Negative Thought. Instantly, in your mind you see yourself walking towards this woman. She greets you, she says she likes you, and you visualize yourself feeling sexy, feeling good, making small talk, flirting your way toward some illicit sexual pleasure. Stop! Disrupt that ANT. Your first action as a *valiant man* is to turn your head away. Well done! You've broken the spell. Now challenge that ANT. Speak to that ANT. Inside your heart or under your breath you get savage and confront that ANT with a positive and determined declaration:

Get out of here, you unworthy idea! You have nothing to do with me! This not my wife! This is my sister! This thought has no place in my life. This is not where my life belongs. I'm a valiant man. I'll die before I dishonor this woman. I'm a man of God and I'm walking on holy ground right now. God, I thank you for my Ewe Lamb and I guard her place in my heart right now!

My friend, you have to take a stand. Confront that ANT and say, *Stop! You don't belong in my head!*

There are different ways in which you can interrupt the automatic flow of those thoughts. Sy Rogers was given some very helpful advice early in his journey to purity of life. A doctor instructed him about the way the brain works and the importance of disrupting those ANTs by deliberately doing a physical action to break the chain and give space to insert a new way of thinking. It sounds so simple you might think it cannot be effective, but the action he adopted to disrupt his ANTs was simply to look at his watch and say, "Well, look at that! It's 8:37." Then a new thought can be inserted: "Lord, bless that woman and bring her to know you." It proved to be enough to disrupt the chain, to turn his thoughts away and allow the inserting of a new thought. You can't stop a thought. You can't say to yourself, *I don't want to think those thoughts!* It's like trying NOT to think about a white elephant. That just doesn't work. You have to disrupt the thought with another thought. You have to stop that chain's progress by starting another chain. Your mind can only think about one thing at a time, so disrupt that ANT and deliberately insert a positive thought.

Douglas Weiss, another expert in this field, speaks highly of the 'Rubber Band' technique.[78] You may be comforted to know that in this technique the rubber band is actually placed around the wrist. A man who wants to break Automatic Negative Thoughts (ANTs)—thoughts that trigger imaginations that run to places you don't need to go—snaps his rubber band in response to every ANT. This helps to disrupt the thought process and sends a signal to the brain to say, *I do not want to stay in this pathway of thinking!* Each time you have an inappropriate, non-relational sexual thought, including a fantasy image, snap that rubber band on your wrist. When you do this, neurologically your brain sees its stimulus, such as a woman, but instead of your brain getting a positive chemical

---

78   D. Weiss, *Sex, Men and God*, Siloam Press, 2002, p. 109.

reinforcement from PEA—or enkephalins and endorphins—it receives a pain stimulus from the snapping of the rubber band. Over the period of about a month, your brain no longer wants to feel the pain of that snapping rubber band each time you sexually objectify a woman, so your brain is reconditioned.

Dr. Weiss, who runs a clinic for men who seriously want to retrain their sexual responses, says the men he has helped claim this technique as the second most effective tool that they were taught in the process of retraining their brains. The most favored and helpful element in their recovery was the support of their wives through the process.

It would be important, however, to recognize that not all therapists are comfortable with the rubber band technique. Others are loathe to associate sexual arousal with pain and thus would choose different ways of interrupting those ANTs... ways that are more cognitive and positive, rather than the negative of a painful intersection.

Regardless of how you decide to go about it, you need to be encouraged by the fact that impulse patterns can be changed in a number of ways, including cognitive therapy. Part of cognitive therapy is talking about the process you're going through, reaffirming your commitment to change, discussing the nature of the change you need to see, and deciding what thought patterns and actions need to be established. At this point, discussion with other men is helpful. This may involve sharing your ideas and your helpful experiences as you grow in sexual maturity. The Valiant Man program involves teaching and small groups for this very purpose.

Using the Bible to retrain your brain

Allowing your Bible to provide you with healthy streams of thought about your sex life is one of the most powerful tools at your disposal in the journey from *good* man to *valiant* man. The Bible is the foundation of all truth. So once you've disrupted your ANT, what are you going to put in its place? What positive, healing, restorative thinking are you going to embrace about sex and sexual responses? Where do you want to take your thought life? Your Bible will provide you with the very best responses. Study key Scripture passages so you understand their intent and learn them by heart. Repeating them with conviction when under pressure is the best place to begin the retraining of your thought world. Choose thoughts that are positive and conform to the Word of God, and let them rip at the slightest provocation. Here are some examples:

You shall not covet your neighbor's wife...[79]

When you find yourself beginning to covet another man's wife, your response must be strong and unequivocal: *I will NOT covet my neighbor's wife. These thoughts are inappropriate. I give them no place in my life. This woman is to be honored and protected. Lust has nothing to do with me!* I speak statements like this to myself out loud. Sometimes, when I find Automatic Negative Thoughts running through my head, I physically stamp my foot and say, *I hate these thoughts! I give them no place in my mind!* And then I'll take a Scripture verse like the ones listed here and begin to speak them out and let their intent touch my emotions.

Drink water from your own cistern, running water from your own well... May your fountain be blessed, and may you rejoice in the wife of your youth. A loving doe, a graceful deer—may her breasts satisfy you always, may you ever be captivated by her love.[80]

---

79   Exodus 20:17
80   Proverbs 5:15, 18-19

In reading verses like this one out loud, I begin to deliberately create a new way of thinking. For instance: *This is my wife! My wife is God's gift to my life!* Then I will say things like, *The Bible says that every good and perfect gift comes down from the Father. God, you gave me this woman. She is your gift to my life. Lord, every good thing is to be found in her. What God has not given to me I don't want. What God has given to me I embrace with thanksgiving, with joy, and with passion. Thank you, Father—she is all I need for this life.*

By speaking and affirming God's Word, I find myself choosing to enter into a relationship with a real woman, a woman about whom I speak positively, with whom I relate tenderly and caringly. I begin to once again see her as a ewe lamb, lovingly nurtured and cherished. This becomes the focus of my attention. You may find it helpful to carry a photograph of your wife around with you, either as she is today or as she was as a child. It will help to remind you of the fact that before God this woman is a precious and priceless gift that God has given you.

In this process I deliberately align my thoughts with God's Word and His perspective, and I declare: *I will not live in a fantasy world with a fantasy woman who is not my wife nor God's gift to my life. Instead, I choose to honor my wife, to love her, and to respect her.* That's how I bring my life back into that ewe lamb mindset.

Here are some more passages from the Bible worthy of being committed to memory. You can add to this list yourself as you read the Bible and encounter passages that speak meaningfully to your journey of purity:

...abstain from ... sexual immorality. You will do well to avoid these things.[81]

So let us put aside the deeds of darkness and put on the armor of light. Let us behave decently, as in the daytime, not in orgies and drunkenness, not in sexual immorality and debauchery, not in dissension and jealousy.[82]

But among you there must not be even a hint of sexual immorality, or of any kind of impurity, or of greed, because these are improper for God's holy people. Nor should there be obscenity, foolish talk or coarse joking, which are out of place, but rather thanksgiving.[83]

Don't be deceived, my dear brothers. Every good and perfect gift is from above, coming down from the Father of the heavenly lights, who does not change like shifting shadows.[84]

Marriage should be honored by all, and the marriage bed kept pure, for God will judge the adulterer and all the sexually immoral.[85]

Flee from sexual immorality. All other sins a man commits are outside his body, but he who sins sexually sins against his own body.[86]

---

81   Acts 15:29
82   Romans 13:12-13
83   Ephesians 5:3-4
84   James 1:16-17
85   Hebrews 13:4
86   1 Corinthians 6:18

But the cowardly, the unbelieving, the vile, the murderers, the sexually immoral, those who practice magic arts, the idolaters and all liars—their place will be in the fiery lake of burning sulfur. This is the second death.[87]

Whatever is true, whatever is noble, whatever is right, whatever is pure, whatever is lovely, whatever is admirable—if anything is excellent or praiseworthy—think about such things.[88]

There have been seasons in my life when I have dedicated myself to the creation of a new brain track and I have written out on a card the attitudes and the truth I desperately need to embrace. I'll pull up at traffic lights and pull that card out of my shirt pocket. In the moments it takes for the red light to turn green, I'll remind myself of those truths, confess them boldly and with passion, then repeat the process at every opportunity during the day. It takes work to go from *good* man to *valiant* man, but you are worth the effort and so are the women and children who look to you for leadership.

The creation of healthy mental tracks in a young man

King Solomon concluded one of his books in the Bible with these powerful words: "*Remember also your Creator in the days of your youth, before the evil days come and the years draw near when you will say, 'I have no delight in them'...*"[89] Some of us reading this book wish with all our hearts that the journey of life had been different with regards our sexuality. Some of us wish that someone

---

87   Revelation 21:8
88   Philippians 4:8
89   Ecclesiastes 12:1

had helped us from our youth to guard our sexuality so that we wouldn't have so much damage to undo.

A *valiant man* cares about raising young men who are equipped to live a successful life because they've been raised with wisdom and understanding. Young men are growing up today in a society riddled with opportunities to develop sexual distortions of every kind. They are not being raised to remember their Creator as they enter puberty and begin to wrestle with that testosterone fog. There is a need for valiant men who understand how to develop pathways of self control and sexual success to invest in the next generation. God wants to see every young man given the opportunity to grow up secure in his sexuality, and with a strong sense of his own value, dignity and destiny.

What issues do fathers, mothers and mentors need to consider in helping young men reach that goal? Keeping in mind that brain tracks are the result of learned behavior, here are some behavioral and environmental conditions that will help to form a pattern for sexual success in a young man's future:

+ The young boy has a masculine brain formed by testosterone. From boyhood to puberty, when the levels of testosterone are low, the young man needs to grow up in an environment where he is neither sexualized nor eroticized. Guard him from those who would engage him in sexual behavior. Allow him his years of innocence. Do not allow his environment to be infected by those who would provoke him to think about sex beyond his level of maturity. In all your conversations about sexual issues keep the issue shame free.

+ In hanging out with other boys, watch how he is accepted and affirmed. Do what you can to ensure he is not growing up with deep feelings of insecurity, feeling that he has to prove something. Help him make it through to puberty without a lot of scars in his life. Give him the privilege of watching his dad relate to his mum with affection and a strong sense of honor. This will allow him to develop a healthy picture of male-female romance, love, commitment and marriage.

+ When puberty hits and his testosterone levels jump by 600 percent, his awareness of girls will be heightened. While he will appreciate the difference between male and female and find himself somewhat attracted to girls, at the same time he will feel a tension or anxiety over the challenge of connecting with a girl romantically. I don't know about you, but I remember those years well. I remember the power that girls had over this young man's emotions. It is a power that can either affirm him or crush him.

+ Talk to him about the tensions of being a teenager. It will help him to identify the fact that a healthy teenage boy is growing up with the following four A's when it comes to relating to girls: Awareness, Appreciation, Attraction and Anxiety. He has already become *aware* of girls. He has already begun to *appreciate* them. He will undoubtedly find himself *attracted* to them and needs to know about the challenge of his own love map and the phenylethylamine experience because it is likely to impact him more than once. Yet, at the same time, he will face the *anxiety* issue over the power that girls can have over his emotions. He needs to be helped to understand the emotional risk he will experience in relation to girls. A girl's approval has the potential to send his emotions through the ceiling and her rejection has the potential to crush his emotions. Help him to deal with it well.

+ In these emotionally dangerous years, key respected males (hopefully including his dad) can affirm the young man and coach him through that challenging period. Having *valiant men* around him can help him to stay clear of damaging eroticism and objectification of girls. Other boys and other men in his life will undoubtedly tell dirty jokes and model a degrading view of women. Dad needs to encourage him. The *valiant men* in his life need to vocalize a very different view of life and model that life to him… with words like:

"Don't go down that pathway, son. A woman is incredibly precious to God, and one day God will give you someone who will think you are a knight in shining armor, someone who will love you and appreciate you for who you are. Don't allow yourself to be drawn into that unhealthy picture of womanhood. Keep yourself away from that kind of thing. There's a bigger picture for your life, son. God has a plan that somebody will love you, and that you will love her in return."

Male mentors in a young man's life

+ Some key male mentor in a young man's life will need to talk to him about the three big issues of fantasy, pornography and masturbation. Hopefully his dad has become a *valiant man* and willingly steps up to play that role. It certainly didn't happen that way in my life. My Dad was a great model in the way he related to my mother and every other woman in his life, but we never had a single conversation that could have helped me develop healthier brain tracks in my own life. If you give that developing young man the right help, he will develop a shame-free self control and a personal dignity about his manhood.

+ A good mentor will coach the young man through those moments of insecurity that undoubtedly occur in the journey of teenage years. He'll need to give him some helpful coaching such as:

"I know it's a scary thing to talk to girls, because they have the power to either humiliate you or make you feel amazing. But don't be afraid. You can manage it. And one day there will be a woman who thinks you are wonderful."

Through that mentoring relationship, the young man can be encouraged to stay sexually clean so he matures with dignity, encouraged that one day he will be able to relate to girls because he is being coached by someone he trusts.

+ One day he will meet a girl and the love map will be triggered. That can happen once or a number of times during a young man's life. If you have a son yourself, my advice to you is to help your son to be aware that those moments are very exciting, but they are also very dangerous.

+ Do not stand by and watch a young man get into a cycle of pairing up with a girl just because the love map has been triggered only to break up and try again a few months later. Jumping into a romantic liaison for a few months only to realize this is not a relationship which is going to end in marriage, disconnecting from the relationship with feelings hurt on both sides of the equation, and then repeating the process over and over again is very unhelpful. That cycle will create a brain track formed on the basis of an immature response to sexuality and create a lifestyle in which he will have difficulty staying committed to a woman beyond the early moments of infatuation. As soon as the infatuation is over, he will feel the relationship is over, and will begin to look for another one.

Fathers and mothers need to coach their children through these moments of early sexual arousal and infatuation. In my teaching series The Search for Intimacy, I lay out five tests which should be applied to assist a young man assess the appropriateness of a developing romance. It could save a young man investing a year of more of his life in a relationship that does nothing more than wound him.

+ Good mentoring will help a young man to treat each young woman he befriends with great respect. Helping him to develop a self control that respects and dignifies every woman he meets is in itself the development of a healthy brain track for a successful life. Then, when he has a green light to proceed to courtship, the relationship can develop beyond friendship with biochemistry reinforcing the process. Testosterone will fuel his sexual desire and focus it on the girl that now fills his dreams. Good counsel and accountability will help him to discipline his increasing desire to touch her and restrain his sexual passions. As a young *valiant man*, he will take whatever steps are necessary to guard and protect her dignity.

+ As the relationship develops and the two relate more closely, the pheromones will kick in. The nasal organs will get involved. The smell of each other's pheromones will begin to connect the body clocks together and their bodies will begin to synchronize. With healthy counsel and wise planning, a wedding is not delayed beyond reasonable boundaries. The Bible says that it is better to marry than to burn.[90] In my opinion, when you have finally found someone you are attracted to and you have a desire to be together, it is unwise to delay their marriage for three, four or five years. In my opinion, that is a fairly unhelpful pathway to walk.

+ For the young man raised in an environment of purity, the first experience of sexual intercourse is in the context of marriage. A profound sense of the privilege of intimacy surrounds the explosion of phenylethylamine as he sees his beloved in her naked glory for the first time. Their sexual bonding is accompanied by the stimulation of all the reward pathways—including endorphins and enkephalins enhanced by the afterglow of oxytocin released through close contact between the happy couple.

+ Every touch reinforces the bond between them and establishes an emotional, behavioral and mental connection for life. The young man has the privilege of living with a focused brain in which the pathways help him to fulfill his calling in life, rather than to resist and divert his calling in life.

In an atmosphere of purity and understanding, this is the hope for the future of every young man. It's not an impossible dream. This is what we have been created for. It's only ignorance and disobedience that has robbed us of our sexual inheritance. This is how a healthy sexual brain is patterned. We can help the next generation do life successfully. We can counsel future generations

---

90   1 Corinthians 7:9

of young men from childhood through to marriage in a way that would be a profound blessing to them and free them from the negative pathways you and I have had to fight in order to live successfully.

The creation of unhealthy mental tracks in a young man

It has been truly said that you can get wounded in this life without trying, but you will not be healthy and well without deliberate application. We've just described the deliberate pathway to healthy sexual brain tracks. But what are the elements involved in the formation of *unhealthy* sexual brain tracks? Well, ignore or reverse any of the steps I have described above and you have the environment for producing an unhealthy sexual groove and a distortion of male sexuality. Here's how it might look:

+ Between childhood and puberty, if you sexualize a child, eroticize a child through abuse, introduce him to pornography, subject him to inappropriate sexual material, or subject him to a sexually destructive family environment, you will have begun the process of training distortions into his life.

+ As he grows, if he is subjected to bullying, rejection, and shame—anything that causes him to feel the pain of being a male—his sexual orientation could be threatened.

+ As puberty kicks in and his libido explodes, a lack of leadership, teaching or mentoring that leaves a young man to find his own way at a time when he is being pressured by emerging passions makes him vulnerable to unhelpful experimentation. His early experiences of sex will lay down brain tracks that will act to direct his reactions in every relationship he enters later in life.

+ The peer group, in the absence of a strong voice for purity in his life, will hold a powerful negative influence over his male development. An environment of shame and silence will isolate him from mature reflection and character development, and the developing distortions will make sexual success in his life harder and harder to achieve.

A young man develops an unhealthy sexual pattern of responses when he pursues sexual activity in one form or another without reference to healthy outcomes or a positive vision for his future. If he doesn't realize that his sexuality is intended to bond him to a woman, that he is meant to love her, cherish her and care for her all the days of his life, and to raise a healthy family with her, the outcome will not be helpful. The tendency for a young man left to himself is to *not* see the big picture. What he sees instead is immediate pleasure, instant gratification, mood-altering opportunities, and all of them play their part in creating unhelpful tracks in his brain. Unhelpful habits have the capacity to take hold of him, fuelled and reinforced by misdirected biochemistry. The tracks in his brain will have formed in response to erotic urgency, and for the rest of his life he will have difficulty staying connected to a woman with all the challenges that true intimacy present.

+ Without significant help, the wounded boy enters into manhood with an array of misbeliefs and bad habits, yet he continues to seek to meet his deep need for intimacy, partnership, acceptance and value. He enters into romantic liaisons, unsure of how to build a great and lasting relationship. His sexual chemistry is not understood. He doesn't understand his conflicting and powerful emotions. With a distorted sexuality he attempts to enter into a marriage but finds it hard to make the relationship work. As a result, women and children around him suffer, and the young man suffers himself.

Confronting self-indulgence, lust, confusion and contradictory attachments will not be easy for this young man. Coming to Christ—or at least taking Christ seriously—will demand such a confrontation.

The need for *valiant men* in this generation is profound. You may not have received the help you needed in your own developing years, and the result may have been a struggle with a variety of distortions you wish you could have avoided. Going from *good* man to *valiant* man takes work. So do the work and make the decision that you will not undertake the journey for yourself alone... for a generation is crying out for the ministry of *valiant men*.

REFLECTION

True meditation means "to mumble". Tell yourself the truth… out loud. Mumble a lengthy passage of Scripture that you know really works for you. There are a number of passages that really do work for me. For example, James chapter one is really important in my life. When I need to reinforce God's Word in my life, I say out loud to myself: *Every good gift comes down from the Father of Life. This is the woman God gave me. This is the woman who is intended by the Father to meet my needs. I choose her. I place my affections on her.* As I do that, I build an off-ramp, and over time this becomes the pathway down which my thoughts run. From that brain center comes a different kind of reward, which we'll talk about in a later chapter.

Meditation is very powerful. The brain chemical GABA (Gamma-aminobutyric acid) is released through meditation. It counteracts the ACh (acetylcholine) and sets up a road block to redirect traffic at the point in the chain that the need to divert from begins. It may be tedious at first, but it will eventually create a new pathway so that life gets easier for you.

I'll never forget the struggle I experienced as a young high school teacher. I had allowed my mind to run down these ANT (automatic negative thought) pathways during my university years, but later as a young Christian, I became distressed at how frequently my thought life was sexually oriented. I remember walking through the classrooms agonizing over this problem I was facing. I didn't realize it then, but what I was doing was building an off-ramp. I was crying out to God, stamping my foot, and declaring I was not willing to allow a place to these unclean thoughts. Sometimes these ANTs would pressure my mind for days at a time. However, as I persisted there came a point at which I could take a stand and say, *No!* And within minutes my mind would be back under control and in a healthier place. Then I could get my thoughts under control within 30 seconds. As I developed new tracks life became a whole lot easier.

Building off-ramps in your brain

So how do you build your off-ramp? Let me summarize the process for you:

1. You have to disturb your ANTs. For example, try using the Rubber Band or the Turning Your Head technique.

2. Then confront those ANTs. Say to yourself out loud: *I give you no place in my mind! You don't belong in my head!*

3. You have got to stamp on those thoughts. Stamp your foot if you can. Declare, *You have no right to exist in my life!*

4. Deliberately speak out God-inspired thoughts. Develop your own confession. Mine went something like this: *God, every good gift comes down from you. My wife is your special gift to me.* If you're not yet married, say, *God, you're the One who is preparing a true answer to my need. God, I'm trusting in you. Lord, I'm going to look to you for the day that you meet that need in my life.*

5. Act on that new thought. Declare it continuously. Do something about it in faith.

6. Reinforce it with an action, a song, a prayer or a confirming statement.

7. Refuse to act on your negative emotions.

8. Repeat it every time that ANT resurfaces and you will bring your ANTs under control. It may take weeks, it may take months, but you will discover yourself falling into a new way of thinking with less and less effort, and less and less struggle.

9. Maintain your accountability. Stay in a process in which you're talking with others about your progress. I encourage men who have undertaken the Valiant Man program to buddy up with the men they began to share with during the program, and to do that for a year in a 'small group' relationship. If you do that with one or two guys, then that's your accountability relationship. A ten week program and a book like this one won't free you of ANTs. In many cases it takes much longer than that. The Valiant Man program and this book will give you a bag full of tools, but it won't complete the process. You need to then start using those tools, and you should stay in an accountability relationship while you learn to apply them.

CHAPTER 8

TAKING A STAND

"Courage is being scared to death—but saddling up anyway."
John Wayne

"To will is to select a goal, determine a course of action that
will bring one to that goal, and then hold to that action till the
goal is reached. The key is action."
Michael Hanson

A common cry from men today is this: "Can somebody help me
bring my thought life under control?" In the last chapter I said
that renewing your mind is not so much a spiritual exercise as it is a
biological or practical exercise. You can't pray to God for a renewed
mind and leave it at that. If you want to bring your thought life under
control, then there is some work to do. It's going to take some effort,
but first you're going to have to understand a little more about the
type of brain you have, and then it's going to require some courage
and willpower for you to take control—to take a stand.

In his book, *Sex, Men and God*, sex therapist Douglas Weiss
identifies three different brain patterns he regularly finds in the
men he deals with. He talks, for example, about the *uni-focused
brain*. A man with a uni-focused brain is a man whose sexual
responses are focused on his wife. Here is a guy who meets a girl,
learns to treasure her, treats her with dignity as their relationship
grows, and makes it to marriage without a heap of baggage.

The first time they experience sexual intercourse is on their
wedding night. Because of his life experiences his brain tracks help
him to be sexually successful without a great deal of conscious
thought. When he is stimulated sexually, his thought life and his
desires run straight to the real woman in his life—his wife—and
he appropriately acts on those passions and on those desires. His
mental development has attached him and bonded him to his wife.
Sexual stimulation leads him to want to care for, love and relate
well to his wife. That's what Weiss calls a uni-focused brain.

Then there's the man who has developed a *dual-focused brain*.
For this man, sexual stimulation during his early years resulted
in some quite different responses. For one reason or another he
developed a relationship with pornography and learned to take
his sexual expression into private places to find stimulation with
pictures. He developed a fantasy sex life that in turn became a

habit, so when he was sexually stimulated his thoughts and mental responses tended to run down that pathway before he had even thought through his responses to certain stimuli. When he is sexually stimulated his thoughts have been trained to move down the fantasy sex pathway.

However, the man with the dual-focused brain has also developed a second pathway. Because he has pursued and cultivated a relationship with a real woman, he has developed a second track in which he has an intimate relationship with his wife that is real and wonderful. Sexual stimulation may produce an appropriate response or an inappropriate response, but when the appropriate response does come, it tends to be diminished in strength. A man with a dual-focused brain may either respond appropriately or head off into a fantasy life, masturbation and/or pornography.

A dual-focused brain does not function as successfully as a uni-focused brain, even when it's on the right track, because it's divided in the way it manages sexual impulses and sexual experiences. Bonding to the right woman is not as easy for this man. He often feels fragmented. Sometimes he feels uneasy about the relationship and he's not sure why he feels that way. That dual track will be a disruptive influence in his life.

Weiss also talks about the man with the *multi-focused brain*. This man has developed more than two habitual responses. He might develop a track that relates to pornography. He might also develop a track in which he objectifies women. He might also develop a track in which women from his past, such as previous girlfriends, live in a fantasy world inside his head. When he's stimulated, sometimes his thoughts run down the pornography track, sometimes they run down the old memory track of past relationships, and in that area of his brain his thoughts cycle around and around. If he's married, his multi-track focus will tend to diminish the strength of the marriage relationship even further than the man with a dual-focused pattern of response. The multi-focused brain has formed a number of learned responses that drain the strength of the response he has to his wife, as sexual energy flows sometimes to pornography, sometimes to the objectification of women, and even to fictional relationships with women from his past.

We have to take the issue of personal purity very seriously. For the woman you married, or will one day marry, you are their one chance in life for the sexual success God intended. If you are struggling with your own sexuality it will be at her expense as well as yours. Now, if that's not a stimulus for you to become a valiant man, it is for me!

Identifying your cyclical behavior

In your quest for personal purity, you need to identify the cycle—if one exists—that allows those tracks in your brain to operate in your life. Addictions are cyclical; fractional addictions might be less developed, but they are still triggered in a similar way and have a similar effect. You need to understand the importance of the trigger points that stimulate your flow of thoughts and set you on a pathway of cyclical behavior.

Those who work in the area of sexual addiction have observed that the cycle tends to begin with obsessive thoughts which produce rising levels of stress. A man may not be fully aware of what he is planning to do, but an obsessive thought bubbles away in his mind, going round and round in his head. This raises the level of stress which in turn triggers a search ritual. This search ritual eventually ignites the flame of sexual activity. Once acted on, the man experiences gratification—he gets what he wants—the flame flares up and then dies away. Sated, he returns to normal, but he feels regret, pain and shame for having acted out. That man may then remain sexually inactive for days or weeks. For a period of time he may tell himself that he's not going to repeat that behavior ever again, but obsessive thoughts will reappear and start the cycle all over again.

This is where self-awareness becomes so important. You cannot change what you have not acknowledged. As you're reading this book, you may have begun to identify some of your own cycles and behaviors. How does the pattern of sexual distortions play out in your own experience? What does the cycle look like for you?

The Book of Proverbs in the Bible provides us with a graphic example of a young man at the front end of just such a cycle. The passage begins in this way:

My son, keep my words
and store up my commands within you. ...

At the window of my house
I looked out through the lattice.

I saw among the simple,
I noticed among the young men,
a youth who lacked judgment.

He was going down the street near her corner,
walking along in the direction of her house

at twilight, as the day was fading,
as the dark of night set in.

Then out came a woman to meet him,
dressed like a prostitute and with crafty intent.[91]

Why accuse the poor guy of lacking judgment? It sounds like all he was doing was going for a walk and some crafty woman trapped him. Not quite! The question this passage ought to raise for you and me is this: What was this young man doing, walking down that part of the street at that time of night? In writing this story, Solomon may well have been reflecting on his own behavioral patterns. He may have drawn this story from personal experience. What Solomon is really saying here is that this was not an entirely accidental event: "Hold on, buddy! Why are you walking down that street? Surely you know who lives down this street and what might happen at this time of night!"

Perhaps this young man was not fully aware of his own habitual patterns. Perhaps he didn't consciously realize that wandering down that street at twilight was the beginning of his search rituals. Then again, perhaps he did. But by allowing himself to walk in a dangerous place at a dangerous time, he walked into a trap.

This is a simple insight from the Bible about the kind of cyclical patterns that we men sometimes allow ourselves to fall into. When obsessive thoughts and desires begin to emerge, we find our feet walking down certain pathways, taking certain actions. The obsessive thoughts cause rising levels of stress or tension, and our search ritual begins.

You and I need to become ruthlessly honest about our habitual patterns, the way in which we tend to let the search begin in our own life. It may be that when you have sexual urges you head to a certain news agency to pick up a newspaper and "accidentally" find yourself checking out porn, or you drive down a particular street,

---

91   Proverbs 7:1,6-10

or you wander down a particular supermarket aisle, or you switch to a more "appealing" television channel. Obsessive thoughts cause tensions which start the search ritual… and we turn to old behavioral habits. Before we've consciously planned a course of action, our mind has arrived at a sexual destination and we simply follow the scent of those obsessive thoughts.

It helps to remind yourself of your goal. Your goal is that you want your eyes, your thoughts, your desires and your emotions—in fact, your whole heart—to be honorable. God has a goal, and his goal sounds something like this: "But among you there must not even be a hint of immorality or of any kind of impurity…"[92] Purity is about sexual gratification coming from nothing or no one but your wife. That's the experience of a man with a uni-focused brain, and that's *our* ultimate goal. Press toward that goal and don't let anything hold you back.

The war we face in our pursuit to become *valiant men* has to be won on three major fronts. And you and I are going to have to become successful in dealing with each one:

1. *Your eyes*—bouncing your eyes off certain images.

2. *Your mind*—learning to capture and evaluate thoughts.

3. *Your heart*—honoring and cherishing womanhood, which above all else includes your wife.

The problem with fantasy

We all have to come to grips with the issue of fantasy—how we think about sex. "What's the problem with fantasy?" you may

93 Ephesians 5:3

well ask. Well, it's very common for men to depend on fantasy for arousal. Men have a population advantage over women in the ability to imagine in three dimensions. That's helpful when it comes to putting an outboard motor back together, but it's a distinct disadvantage when fantasy—in terms of imagined sexual encounters—hijacks your purity of heart. Men are very much influenced by fantasy, which is not essentially wrong if the content of that thought life—what you're thinking about sexually—is appropriate and if the fantasy itself is not inherently unclean.

However, here is one of the biggest issues you have to face about fantasy: Fantasy is not reality, even if it's about the woman to whom you are married. You need to recognize that the more you retreat into fantasy, the more you retreat from a real relationship with a real person, and that's what you're alive for. Fantasy is doing life that isn't real. It's about doing life in your imagination. Fantasy can be an avoidance of the real world and that in itself is a problem. You are created to relate, to be intimate, and to share your life with a real person in a real world, not live in a pretend world that does not exist outside of your own brain cells.

The second reason why fantasy is wrong is that it's addictive. The more you practice it, the more you need it, and so you drift further from reality. The third reason why fantasy is wrong is that it leads to acting out in our lives. A fourth problem with fantasy is that men frequently have intrusive sexual thoughts. These thoughts can take place anywhere and at any time. Now, I don't know about you, but I've been stunned at the inappropriate places that sexual thoughts can suddenly intrude into my conscious world. It's happened to me in the middle of a church worship service. Fantasy gives those inappropriate and intrusive thoughts a nest to sit in. It allows those thoughts to set up residence in your head and form brain tracks that become distressingly habitual.

For these four very good reasons you have to deal decisively with inappropriate fantasy in your life. Do all you can to ensure that the only fantasy you do have is limited to appropriate imagination. A perfectly healthy fantasy may involve your anticipation of a birthday party, or a holiday, or a new car. You may spend time thinking about those things… about how you'll feel, what color you would like, and the conversations you'll have. But when you begin to lose contact with real life because you're lost inside your own head, that is no longer appropriate, and you need to be ruthless about bringing yourself back out of that fantasy life and into real life.

The problem with pornography

Some men will ask, "What's the problem with pornography?" Dr. Archibald Hart rightly says many men have a love-hate relationship with pornography; they love the feelings it gives them, but they hate the shame and the uncleanness that follows. This may be obvious to you, but it's still important to state it clearly: There is a strong link between fantasy and pornography. Remember, men think visually. Men are drawn to pictures, especially pictures of nudity or sexual activities. The ready availability of visual stimulation in our society is changing the way men think and behave. And the change is definitely not helpful.

So what are the problems with pornography? Well, it causes men to prefer a fantasy woman over a real woman. In comparison to pornographic sex, real sex with a real woman can be a challenge for any man. I believe that ought to be said more often. One of the things I regret most about growing up as a man in my generation is that because we didn't receive sexual discipleship, we had little realistic insight to the whole issue of sex and marriage. Nobody ever told me about what to expect on my honeymoon. In a man's fantasy world, honeymoons are unending experiences of sexual bliss. But the reality is that batteries only last so long, and after you've had two or three orgasms, the fact is that sex becomes tiring. If nobody tells you that, you can feel pretty inadequate when reality sets in.

I remember experiencing feelings of claustrophobia during my honeymoon. Courting was both thrilling and emotionally exhausting, but at least at the end of a night I could drop her off and go home. On our honeymoon nobody was going home. One day, while Helen was in our apartment, I headed to a supermarket and walked up and down the aisles just to be alone by myself for a while. It bugged the daylights out of me because I was experiencing feelings nobody had told me to expect. *What's the matter with me?* I began to ask myself: *Is there something wrong with me? Is this normal?* I've since learned that honeymoons are often very difficult experiences. Mine wasn't, but some of the feelings I had were unexpected and more problematic than I was been prepared for.

The fact is that sex with a real woman can be problematic, at least sometimes. In chapter six we discovered that every man must learn that a woman's sexuality is way more complex than his own. She is affected by factors that are insignificant to a man, such as the rising and falling levels of hormones in her body. In comparison, testosterone in a man stays relatively constant. A man simply does not know what it feels like to go through life as a woman. This means that attempting to be sexual with a woman can sometimes be difficult, tiring, and even hurtful when what starts out romantically ends up in an argument. Sex requires considerable communication skills at times, and even then it doesn't always turn out as hoped or expected.

The sad consequence is that a man can come to the conclusion that it is easier to get sexual satisfaction from a pretend woman rather than from a real woman. For a man, the challenge of truly loving, caring for and pleasing a woman is a significant one. One of the dangers is that a man can begin to prefer a fantasy woman over a real woman. A man can move from the challenge of a real relationship, with a real person, to a relationship with a piece of paper covered in millions of colored ink dots. He discovers that a piece of paper does not throw unexpected challenges at him. He gets the same result from a piece of paper and from masturbation every time. And sadly for some men they find it so challenging to have a safe experience with a real woman in real life that a fantasy woman becomes preferable. Fantasy is far less challenging and requires way less effort and commitment. As a result, it's not hard for a man to develop a dual-focused or a multi-focused brain, taking some of that sexual energy and training it down a very different but unhelpful pathway.

Pornography substitutes intimacy with sexual excitement

Another serious problem with pornography is that it teaches a man to substitute sexual excitement for intimacy. Intimacy is more challenging and difficult for a man. Intimacy requires effort, talk and emotion. Sexual excitement requires none of that. That's why some men prefer to substitute sexual excitement for intimacy. However, you and I were created for intimacy with a measure of sexual excitement attached. Pornography is a robber, and we need to make a decision that we're not going to be robbed of the privilege of intimacy in our lives.

A third problem with pornography is its impact on young minds, especially during those formative years when sex-related tracks are being formed in the brain. Some men describe the impact of pornography in their early years as "the beginning of their struggle to maintain sanity".[93] When young men first engage in sexual activity,

93   Hart, p. 87.

it impacts them with incredible force. The relentless pressure for sex that can be generated by pornography inside a young man's head can tip a young man into a place where he feels like he's going insane. Erotica viewed prior to the age of fourteen produces a more sexually active adult and causes a man to become engaged in more and varied sexual behaviors as a result.[94]

The fourth problem with pornography is that it is addictive. Pornography gives a thrill as brain chemistry is stimulated, but neurochemical tolerance will eventually kick in and draw a man to heavier and more regular pornography, even as a drug addict finds himself needing more and more of a drug to get his kicks. This leads to another problem with pornography: As a man engages in pornography, and the pressure rises to move onto more dramatic levels of pornography, women become dehumanized and objectified in his mind. Pornography pushes that tendency in a man way down the track and causes him to see women as objects, as things. Over time, pornography teaches a man that his wife is a three-dimensional piece of pornography, and that, my friend, has to be confronted. It's not only destructive to a man's progress toward becoming a *valiant man* it's thoroughly demeaning to a woman and an intolerable affront to her dignity.

Finally, pornography damages marriages. Research has shown that men and women exposed to pornography universally rate their spouse less attractive because of the experience. They also noted that they feel less in love with their spouse. Zillman and Bryant researched this tendency and noted:

> … repeated exposure to pornography results in a decreased satisfaction with one's sexual partner, with the partner's sexuality, with the partner's sexual curiosity, a decrease in the valuation

94   N. Malamuth and E. Donnerstein, *Pornography and Sexual Aggression*, Academic Press, p. 7.

of faithfulness, and a major increase in the importance of sex without attachment. [95]

Dr. Victor Cline, a professor of psychology and a noted researcher and counselor in the area of the effects of pornography, states:

> In the scientific world, the question of pornography and its effects is no longer a hot issue. It's really not debated anymore. The scientists and professionals are no longer 'pretending not to know'. The new pornography commission is almost redundant. Everybody knows that pornography can cause harm, it can also change people's sexual appetites, values and behavior... It's a power form of education. It can also condition people into deviancy. It can also addict. There are too many articles in the scientific journals as well as current books reviewing research attesting to this for anybody to deny its effects anymore.[96]

In light of the above, if you're a person who has any faith in God at all, and if you believe we are in a spiritual environment and our sexuality has a spiritual component, you need to see pornography as a cursed object. You cannot view pornography without entering a demonically-charged zone. This is one of the reasons why pornography has such a powerful impact on people. To own it or to view it is to loiter in a demonically-charged zone.

The Bible says:

> The images of their gods you are to burn in the fire. Do not covet the silver and gold on them, and do not take it for

95   D. Zillman and J. Bryant, 'Pornography, Sexual Callousness, and the Trivialization of Rape', *Journal of Communications* 32, 1982, p. 15.

96   www.unitedfamilies.org/hibbert9.asp

yourselves, or you will be ensnared by it, for it is detestable to the Lord your God. Do not bring a detestable thing into your house or you, like it, will be set apart for destruction. Utterly abhor and detest it, for it is set apart for destruction.[97]

My friend, today is the day you need to say to yourself and to God, "This just has to stop in my life!" Even if you're not successful in bringing this to an end in one day, it's important that you appreciate the significant role that pornography plays in destroying the purity of a man's heart and make a decision that you are going to be rid of it.

The problem with masturbation

The problem of pornography increases as you add it to the issue of masturbation. What does the Bible teach about masturbation? Well, we saw in chapter five that there is possibly only one verse in the Bible that seems to speak directly to this subject[98], and I believe it encourages us not to attach unnecessary shame to the act of masturbation. In other words, an experience of masturbation is not intended to be a shame-filled event in a man's life. I don't think the Bible attaches the same connotation of shame that *we've* tended to attach to masturbation.

However, that doesn't mean that masturbation is helpful, or that it may not have a significant impact on a man's purity. Douglas Weiss identifies six levels of behavior as men relate to masturbation.[99] Now, you may feel that the experiences you've had with masturbation are not serious or significant, but you need to ask

---

97   Deuteronomy 7:25-26
98   Leviticus 15:16
99   D. Weiss, *Sex, Men and God*, Siloam Press, 2002, pp. 75-92.

yourself this question: *Which of the following six categories do I fit into?*

1. **Some men never masturbate:** Some men completely leave masturbation alone; they never go there. In Western civilization, it is estimated that perhaps four percent of the masculine population fits in this category. However, in some cultures where masturbation is seen as something only weak men do, the majority of men do not take part in masturbation.

2. **Connected and occasional:** A second way in which men relate to masturbation is that they do it occasionally while staying connected to themselves and to the real world. In other words, they don't use pornography. Masturbation for this group is not about lust or sexual fantasies, it's more like a bodily function as a reaction to physiological pressure. This is especially true of teenagers when they discover that the penis is pleasurable and that masturbation is enjoyable. Their experience may be simply about physical pleasure or about obtaining a physical release.

    If I look back on my experience of masturbation, I would fit into this category. Fortunately, because it wasn't available to me, pornography was not a part of my life. So I never connected masturbation with pornography. In my experience, starting around the age of twelve, masturbation was simply a thrilling experience. It was the most fun you could have at the age of twelve without owning a rifle or being allowed to drive a car. In my experience, it wasn't about lust or anything else other than the fact that I had found a very pleasant way to manage my own body.

    A man in this category ends his experience with masturbation after he gets married. For him, there is no longer any point to it. Marriage ends masturbation, except in situations in which his wife is ill or pregnant, or if there is prolonged separation when sex is not possible. In those circumstances, masturbation may occur as a physical release of a physiological pressure. From my study of the Bible, I believe that while you may not want to encourage frequent masturbation, there should be no shame attached to it in those specific situations.

3. **Connected and regular:** The third way that men can relate to masturbation is that while they stay connected to the real world, they masturbate on a very regular basis. For men in this category, it's more frequent than occasional. For them, it isn't about altering moods or about fantasy or pornography, but it's still a regular activity. It may continue long after marriage and may divert considerable sexual energy from the marriage relationship.

4. **Disconnected binge:** The fourth way in which men relate to masturbation is that they disconnect from the real world and enter into a fantasy experience. While they are masturbating they enter an imaginary world or live out an inner visualization or fantasy. Disconnected binge masturbators stay away from it for periods of time, but then there is intense activity that might go on for a few days or for a week before it stops again. However, when masturbation occurs it's about fantasy and getting lost in a trip inside the head. During masturbation the man visualizes a story or a picture in his mind. This category of masturbation is about the fulfillment of a fantasy life, pornography or a mood-altering escape.

5. **Disconnected and regular:** In describing the fifth way in which men relate to masturbation, Weiss talks about men who

are disconnected, lost in a fantasy world, and who masturbate regularly. For this group it is not uncommon for more masturbation to be going on than sex with their wives.

6. **Disconnected and addicted:** The sixth level involves men who are disconnected from the real world as they masturbate to fantasy, pornography, and to the life inside their head. As well as this their behavior is driven and expressive of sexual addiction; they are aware that their behavior is out of control.

The effects of masturbation on your brain patterns

A healthy man has a uni-focused brain. That's where you and I are headed. The *valiant man* seeks to live in a place where his sexual behavior and fulfillment are all focused on the treasure that God has given him in his wife. A healthy man has a uni-focused brain that stays in the real world. It isn't diverted by fantasy. He finds his fulfillment in the reality of marriage. The whole focus of his experience is a real relationship with a real woman.

When a man develops a dual-focused or a multi-focused brain, he finds himself disconnecting from reality to engage with fantasy or objectification, turning a woman into a sex object. A man with a dual-focused or a multi-focused brain is sexually fractured. Intimacy is diminished and bonding is disturbed, with the result that relationships become difficult for this man.

Those who relate to masturbation in levels 4, 5 or 6 (described above) are training their brain to be dual-focused or multi-focused. Their behavior is creating a double track. Sometimes sexual stimulation leads to a lonely sexual fulfillment in a fantasy world, and sometimes it results in a healthy relationship with the woman God has given them.

If you recognize yourself in level 4, 5 or 6, then you need to confront it. You need to realize that you are diverting your sexual energy into a lonely act of self indulgence. In some ways you are training yourself to be dual-focused in the sense that you are diverting your sexual energy down a second pathway. If you find yourself in level 3, you need to ask yourself: *Why am I doing this?* You need to ask yourself if perhaps you still consider sex to be the meaning of life. Think about it. My friend, it's time to say to yourself: *This needs to change! This needs to stop!*

The power of your will

In order to change, you need to build an off-ramp. As I have said before, once a track is formed in your brain, it will be with you for the rest of your life. Tracks can't be simply eradicated, but you can divert them and build new ones so that the unhealthy tracks don't affect your sexuality and your behaviors as they once did. Build a new one and stick with it, and you'll find the old tracks will fade in time and their impact on your life will diminish to an echo. A key to the building of new and healthy tracks is the power of your will.

Unexpected and intrusive unclean thoughts can be distressing. Every man needs to be aware of the fact that it simply goes with the territory of being a male. You cannot stop intrusive thoughts popping into your head from time to time. However, you *can* learn the skill of redirecting your thoughts, deciding to think about other things, and turning your thoughts deliberately to healthy places. ANTs will either ruin your life or run your life until you learn the skill of renewing your mind and exercising it regularly. And this process will demand an exercise of your will.

If you're going to build an off-ramp, it's going to require that you take a stand, and this is where the role of your will comes into the equation. One of the most important factors in becoming a *valiant man* is appreciating the fact that you have a will and learning to use it. The power of your will is not so much about white-knuckling it through life and trying to stop yourself from reacting to temptation. It's more about choosing to do the positive things you are learning to do in order to create new brain tracks, and it's about choosing to stick with the program under pressure.

Where does the ability to "will" come from? Within our humanity there exists an element that goes beyond our body, our desires, our biochemistry, and even our brain wiring. It's called the spirit. At the core of every human life is spirit. Spirit is a non-material form of life; it's not made up of atoms and molecules, cells and chemical compounds. The spirit has the capacity to set a direction and choose a course of action despite every contrary voice. Your brain tracks may say, "Let's do it!" Your body may say, "Let's do it!" Your biochemistry may say, "Let's do it!" And your emotions may say, "Let's do it!" Yet there is a power with the human spirit that has the ability to defy all else and to say, "No! I want to do something different! I want to choose a different direction!" Your will is an exercise of your human spirit and it gives you the ability to choose a certain direction, even when all the other voices are crying out for you to go a different way.

My friend, you will not grow in personal purity without exercising your will, and anyone who has tried to exercise their will knows that it is a battle. As a man, sexual conflict will be with you for the rest of your life, but you can become stronger and increasingly successful at managing it by learning how to exercise your will.

Sexual conflict within a man emanates from a number of sources. You experience conflict when the society around you pushes you and provokes you to be sexually active in ways that are destructive to you. Sexual conflict also originates from within your own body. Your testosterone-driven masculinity wants sex at times that is inappropriate and with inappropriate people. Your thoughts are a source of sexual conflict; a sexual thought can run straight to the end of a brain track, provoking a desire to take action long before you've made a decision to do so. At the same time, your emotions can be crying out, "Oh, I feel lonely! Oh, I deserve a little excitement in life! I'd like to experience some sexual satisfaction! Maybe I can do it and get away with it!" As a man, you will regularly face sexual conflict at the emotional level.

All those voices are not a problem if they happen to align themselves with what is appropriate, but all too often they will be against you because the actions they will provoke are not appropriate. Regardless, in the middle of it all, you have a spirit that gives you the ability to make a contradictory choice. That's what marks you as different from an animal. Dogs have sex whenever their hormones direct them. However, when your hormones direct you to have sex, you can maintain self-control. You can be moved by a vision of what is true and noble and right. That's what makes us different from every other animal on the face of the earth. We have the ability to assess the appropriateness, the rightness and the goodness of an action. You and I do not have to be driven by our environment, our biochemistry, our body, our thoughts or our feelings. We need to realize that it's the spirit that has the power to will and to exercise choice. That's the power of the human spirit within you.

So why can't we all just commission our spirit to make the right choices and live godly, pure lives? Why isn't it as easy as that? Well, sometimes it is. All of us have probably come to moments of conflict in life where we made a decision to do the right thing, and when we did we won a small victory. Those victories have the power to inspire us and change us so that we face future conflicts with a higher level of confidence.

I had one of those remarkable "change" moments some years ago. I was on long service leave with Helen and we'd just arrived in Singapore. I was walking down a street when I made this decision: "I'm never going to bite my finger nails again!" Up to that moment, I had bitten my nails all my life. Since that day I have never bitten my nails again. I just decided to start clipping them. I made a decision: "I'm not doing this anymore!" And a habit of a lifetime was broken, simply because I made a decision to exercise the power of my will.

Your willpower alone won't help you

Why isn't it as easy as that for every problem in life? The answer is this: Because our will (our human spirit) was not designed to function in isolation. Our human spirit was designed to be married to the Spirit of God. It was God's intention that in the intimacy of the marriage of our human spirit to His Spirit, our desires would be influenced and encouraged by the desires of the Holy Spirit. It was God's design that in intimacy with His Spirit, your will would be healthy.

Now here's the problem: You and I were never designed to exercise our will in isolation from the Spirit of God. We are broken human beings, damaged by the fall described in the Bible[100], and we have to realize that our spirit has been damaged along with every other part of us. Our inner most being, the spirit within us, is not perfect and holy; it's damaged like the rest of us. While it's true that possessing a human spirit gives us the power to choose, it's also true that our spirit can only choose as well as a wounded spirit can choose. We may well say to ourselves, *Oh well, I have free will, so I can make any choice I want.* If you've ever tried to lose weight or stop smoking or even start reading the Bible more often,

---

100   Genesis chapter 3.

you will often have found yourself failing over and over again. A wounded spirit trying to choose the right thing in isolation from God's Spirit will all too often fail.

There was a man in the Bible who wrote in the Book of Romans about his own struggle with his will. He said, "The good stuff that I want to do, I don't seem to be able to do, and the bad stuff I don't want to do, I find myself doing it over and over again. What is going on?"[101] (My translation of this Scripture) Well, that is evidence of our damaged will at work.

If our spirit is polluted, it can only *will* as well as a polluted spirit can will. If it is bruised or wounded, it can only *will* as well as a bruised or a wounded spirit can will. That's why bringing Jesus Christ into your struggle is the most important step that you will ever make. You see, Jesus said this:

"Come to me, all you who are weary and burdened, and I will give you rest. Take my yoke upon you and learn from me, for I am gentle and humble in heart, and you will find rest for your souls. For my yoke is easy and my burden is light.[102]

Jesus said, "Behold, I stand at the door and knock. If anyone hears my voice and opens the door, I will come in to him and eat with him, and he with me."[103] Your human spirit is at the core of your power to become a *valiant man*, but your human spirit needs to be fortified and supported by a partnership with the Spirit of Christ. Your spirit needs to be yoked to the power of God's Spirit. In partnership with God's Holy Spirit, a new life can unfold. Your will is a key to the future, but your will was never designed to function apart from the presence, healing and support of God's Spirit.

---

101   Romans 7:15-17
102   Matthew 11:28-30
103   Revelation 3:20, ESV

It's time to humble yourself and relax into a partnership with God as you continue on your journey from *good* man to *valiant* man.

REFLECTION

If you will let Jesus into this struggle over your sexuality, He will step in and be your strength. Begin to honestly say to Him, "I have challenges and today I want to make some important decisions. I've made them before, but I tend to fail. Jesus, please come in and join your strength with my strength. Help me to *will* what I need to will."

How can you practically engage in a partnership with the Holy Spirit? Let me explain just one way that has been life changing for me. Some time ago, I was struggling with emotions and desires that just weren't helpful. A lot of emotional energy was being spent every day just keeping myself in check and I knew I needed the Holy Spirit to strengthen my human spirit and realign my will. I woke up around 4:00 am on a number of mornings, went into my living room, put on some worship music, and lay out on the carpet. During those times I just exposed my heart to the presence of God. I didn't say a lot, I just lay there and opened my heart to Jesus and relaxed in his presence with a prayer: "Here I am. Heal my emotions and make your will my will." I'd stay there until dawn and just rest my heart in his presence. I can't explain to you why this works except for the promise of Jesus: "If anyone opens the door I will come in and sup with him and he with me." Without a big fight and a lot of fuss, those moments changed me. I found myself living without a war going on inside me, and all I can say is, "I'm grateful!"

Chapter 9

Guarding Your Heart

"You don't love a woman because she is beautiful, but she is
beautiful because you love her."
Anonymous

"When the heart has acquired stillness, it will look upon the
heights and depths of knowledge, and the intellect, once quieted,
will be given to hear wonderful things from God."
Hesychios the Martyr

One of the three major areas in which a man must do battle for personal purity is his heart. The first two areas we've explored so far are the eyes and the mind. We've talked about the importance of guarding our eyes and learned the necessity of bouncing our eyes away from images that stimulate the sexual chemistry in our head. We've talked about the importance of learning to guard our thought life; to identify unhelpful brain tracks and retrain the brain by deliberately developing off-ramps and learning to create new and healthy tracks.

Your heart is the third domain that needs your careful attention. You and I need to protect, corral and guard our hearts in our journey to becoming *valiant men*. Why the heart? What's so significant about the heart? Well, your heart is the wellspring of all your affections, motivations and desires. The Bible puts it this way: "Above all else, guard your heart, for it is the wellspring of life."[104] That's why you will want to guard it. That's why you will want to bring your heart and its affections to a place of purity. Life is a lot less stressed when your heart is aligned with God's purposes. Your life is at peace when that which flows up out of your desires, your passions and your longings is aligned with what is right and what is appropriate.

Before I unravel the truths about how to guard your heart, I want to tell you a story. It will help to underline what we've been learning about renewing the mind, off-ramps and new brain tracks. During the study process to create the Valiant Man program, I had an opportunity to share some of the material I was learning with a group of Christian ministers. I explained to them that one of the most important keys I had learned about renewing the mind is that it is not essentially a spiritual process which results from an answer to prayer, rather it is a biological process which

104   Proverbs 4:23

results from appropriate behaviors. In other words, if you do the appropriate work, the brain can be retrained; but if you don't do the appropriate work, prayer alone won't do it for you. One of the ministers present connected that insight with his own experience and was transparent enough to share his story. It's a great example of how off-ramps and new brain tracks are formed and how they can change your life.

He had grown up in a family with three boys where the dad had never given them an ounce of sexual discipleship. He had developed a habit of masturbation in his life which dramatically escalated when he encountered pornography. When he had come to know Christ and began attending church, he hated the tension between the old habits and the call to a new life of purity and freedom. One day he was standing in front of a news agency window and a picture triggered those old brain tracks. A flood of unclean thoughts and desires followed. He was so distressed that he cried out, "God, You have got to show me how I can change this!" There was an immediate response to his cry as this thought clearly surfaced in his mind: "Whenever you have unclean thoughts, I want you to praise me as the Creator of the heavens and the earth." It was clear and it was practical, so from that moment he began to do it. Every time he was aware of an unclean thought, he would interrupt that thought, he would divert it, and he would say, "No, God is the Creator of the heavens and the earth!" And he would follow up with a deliberate stream of pure and uplifting thoughts of worship and thanksgiving. He chose to underline that behavior by deliberately meditating on this thought: *God is the Creator of heaven and earth and He has created my wife. He has brought her into my life as my provision. And I love her and commit myself to her.*

In this book I have been using the terms "off- ramp" and "brain tracks" to describe the process involved in renewing the mind.

What this minister did is a good example of an off-ramp followed by the building of a whole new brain track. His off-ramp was an act of praise to God. Then a whole new track was formed along the lines of appreciation, honor and thanksgiving. Over a period of time, he successfully intercepted every one of those ANTs and diverted his thoughts down the new track he built by bold, positive confessions activated by a deliberate exercise of his will. As a result, he found himself living a different kind of life and he is enjoying the fruit of his warfare to this day.

The creation of new and healthy thought processes is crucial if you want to develop new brain tracks, and these thought processes become the fences you will need to guard and maintain a pure heart.

The Bible says:

Therefore, I urge you, brothers, in view of God's mercy, to offer your bodies as living sacrifices, holy and pleasing to God—this is your spiritual act of worship. Do not conform any longer to the pattern of this world, but be transformed by the renewing of your mind.[105]

If you value your life and your marriage, bring your heart back to the place of purity; then guard it, surround it and encircle it with purity. Left to itself, your heart can very easily develop the nature of a donkey in heat—when you are stimulated through your eyeballs the outcome is junk sex. We all need to learn to corral the heart, to reign in our affections and desires, and take this stand: *My heart and its passions are not going to simply run wild and do whatever they want. I am going to bring my heart back to a place where it was intended to be.*

---

105   Romans 12:1-2

Eight principles to corral the heart of a *valiant man*

To help you guard your heart, I want to give you eight principles derived from the Bible that will assist you to create new thoughts, new desires and new commitments. These eight principles will help you to guard your emotions and your passions. So here are eight principles to corral the heart of a *valiant man*.

Principle 1: If God doesn't give it to me, I don't want it

In the New Testament, James gives us some valuable insights to the whole problem of temptation:

When tempted, no one should say, "God is tempting me." For God cannot be tempted by evil, nor does he tempt anyone; but each one is tempted when, by his own evil desire, he is dragged away and enticed.[106]

The word translated *enticed* in this passage carries the idea of "bait". When you want to catch a trout, you've got to get bait that looks attractive to the trout; bait that looks like food, smells like food, and tastes like food. If a trout has a strong desire for worms, you've got to put a worm on that hook. A trout swimming around with a strong desire for worms will see your worm dangling in the water and say to himself: *That's what I've been looking for!* He then bites the worm and gets caught, because inside that worm is a hook. You see, that succulent-looking worm wasn't a provision of God at all! It was very cunningly constructed bait, and bait is nothing less than a trap for unsuspecting trout.

The word translated as *evil desire* in this passage is the Greek word *epithumea*, which really means "strong desire". Strong desires

---

106   James 1:13-14

aren't necessarily evil, but they do set you up to be vulnerable to bait. What James is saying in this passage is this: "You've got to be careful, because your strong desires can be baited." Masturbation, fantasy and pornography can look like the real thing, smell like the real thing, and taste like the real thing, but they *aren't* the real thing. The real thing is real intimacy with a real woman with whom you have a covenantal commitment. The "strong desire" in our heart is for *pericoresis*[107], bonding and true connection. Now, bait can look, smell and taste fantastic, but if it has a hook in it, you're going to be trapped and deeply disappointed. That's why James goes on to say:

> Then, after desire has conceived, it gives birth to sin; and sin, when it is full-grown, gives birth to death. Don't be deceived, my dear brothers. Every good and perfect gift is from above, coming down from the Father of the heavenly lights, who does not change like shifting shadows.[108]

God is the only One who gives you food every time. He doesn't feed you bait. If you go for bait, the chances are you will find yourself hooked and dragged away. So always be aware that if God didn't provide it for you, it will prove to be a trap, no matter how attractive it looks. Did God provide a fantasy life to meet your needs? The answer is "No!" God provided you with a real woman in a real world to have a real relationship in a real covenant. God's provision for you is your wife, with no hook attached. So don't go to fantasy and pornography to meet your needs, because they come from hell.

Pornography is a device designed to capture and ensnare

---

107   If you've forgotten what this word means, go back to Chapter Four
       and refresh your memory.
108   James 1:15-17

men. A man is created for real intimacy with a real woman, so it doesn't make sense for a man's heart to be glued to a piece of paper with ink dots all over it. It's really hard to have intimacy with a piece of paper! That's called deception. The Bible says, "Don't be deceived!"[109] The only provision that will meet your need is what God provides for you. By the way, if you're a single man, wait until God provides an answer to your need.

This has become a very powerful truth that has captured my heart. When tempted, I declare to myself: *I'm not going to be baited and hooked! I'm hanging out for the real thing. What God provides is the real thing.* That's why God encourages us to aim for a uni-focused brain, one that refuses to latch onto anything except the real thing that God has provided for us. The Bible says, "For this reason a man will leave his father and mother and be united to his wife, and the two will become one flesh."[110] You have one wife to cling to, one wife to love, and one wife to cherish. So receive her as a gift from God and recognize that nothing else is real; everything else is bait. Embracing that truth has the power to guard your heart.

When it comes to other women in this world you and I are counseled by our Father in heaven to have this attitude: "Treat … older women as mothers, and younger women as sisters, with absolute purity."[111] There are some things you just don't do with your sister. You and I are encouraged by James to have one wife, many mothers and many sisters. View the older women in your life as mothers. View the younger women in your life as sisters. You and I are called to have one wife. That is a uni-focused brain. Get that thought track strongly ingrained in your mind. My friend, if

---

109 James 1:16
110 Mark 10:7-8
111 1 Timothy 5:1-2

you're not yet married, prepare yourself for marriage by embracing this truth in a pure and honest heart: *If God doesn't provide it, I don't want it!*

Principle 2: I am thankful for what God has given me

The last of the Ten Commandments deals with a vital attitude for guarding your heart: "You shall not covet your neighbor's house. You shall not covet your neighbor's wife, or his manservant or maidservant, his ox or donkey, or anything that belongs to your neighbor."[112] Most of us have probably never knowingly coveted a neighbor's ox, but I'd suspect that most of us have coveted most of the other things on that list. This is a very important principle to understand. Covetousness means looking over the fence at somebody else's grass and believing it really is greener; that if only you could get over the fence and get what your neighbor has, at last your heart would be satisfied. A *valiant man* knows that the grass is really greener where it has been watered properly.

Now, the way the devil uses this is fascinating. In fact, he used this principle to destroy the world way back in the beginning. The devil entered the garden where God had given our mum and dad everything, with the exception of one tree. God told them, "Everything is yours. The whole world is yours. The garden is yours. But this one tree is mine."

Then that creep came slithering into the garden and said to Eve, "Has God told you that you can't touch anything in the garden?"

To which she replied, "No! We're allowed to have lots of things. In fact, everything in the garden is ours. But there is one thing we have been told not to touch."

---

112   Exodus 20:17

The devil responded, "Aw, sorry to have to tell you this, but you see, that's the key to your happiness. If only you could have that one thing you were told not to touch, you would find perfect fulfillment."

So Mum climbed the fence to go pick that fruit off a tree that didn't belong to her. And Dad followed. Then suddenly they discovered it wasn't the key to perfect happiness at all. Instead, they had destroyed their integrity and destroyed their relationship with God.

Are you content with what God has provided you? The word *contentment* means "to dwell within limits". The devil will come to you and say, "How can you be happy if you have a limited life? You can't be happy if you live a limited life!"

But God says, "I want you to dwell within limits." Remember how it was back there in the Garden of Eden? God said, "I give you all of this, but don't touch that one thing." You see, the only unlimited person in the universe is God Himself. You and I are *meant* to have limits.

Part of the key to our success in life is learning to live within the limits that God has given us. Now, you're allowed to ask God to expand your limits, but when it comes to women, God has a limit for you: You only get one. So you need to dwell within your limits. Discontent is a powerful driver to a multi-focused sexuality. Discontent says, "How can I ever be fulfilled having just one focus for my sexuality?" Well, it's the only way you will ever be fulfilled. Discontent looks over the fence to someone else's provision and perceives greener grass. Discontent fuels a fantasy for what is *not* real, and it fuels repugnance for what *is* real.

Today, you and I need to adopt this attitude and speak it out: *I refuse to dishonor myself, my God and my wife by coveting other women. God has given me all that I need for a wonderful life. I am blessed and I am grateful for God's provision in my life.*

The Bible says, "But if we have food and clothing, we will be content with that."[113] The Bible also says, "But godliness with contentment is great gain."[114] The key to contentment is to focus on the good things you have. Do you realize that the moment your wife has to compete with every other woman in the world, you can find a million things wrong with her? When the directors were shooting the movie *Pretty Woman*, they couldn't even use all of Julia Roberts. They had to use somebody else's hands and someone else's legs in key sections of the movie, because Julia Roberts is not the perfect woman. So when it came to featuring a pretty woman in his movie, the movie director couldn't just have one woman—he had to have a number of different women combine their beauty into one pretty woman.

So when you demand that your wife compete with every other woman in the world, it's a contest no woman can ever win. If you're going to do what God is asking you to do—to dwell within your limits and cherish just one woman—you're going to need to stop beating her up for what she isn't and treasure her for what she is. If I judge my wife for what she isn't, she can't win. But if I treasure her for what she is, and value her for what she is, then inside that limit I can have a real life. She can't be everything, but she sure is something! God tells us that that is one of the great keys to success in life.

My friend, today make a decision that you will be rabidly and outrageously grateful for what God has given you, and that you'll continue to be grateful all the days of your life. If you will do that today, it will release a great blessing in your household. Guard your heart with this principle: She sure is something, and I'm forever grateful.

---

113   1 Timothy 6:8
114   1 Timothy 6:6

Principle 3: What God has given me is profoundly valuable

A wife is a miracle of incalculable dimensions. She is a miracle; a person created in the image of God with dreams, hopes, needs, likes, dislikes, passions, creativity and so much more. To be given the privilege of life with a wife is a gift beyond measure. My prayer is that I prove myself worthy by honoring and serving her all the days of her life.

This revelation changed my life. The revelation that every woman is a miracle—that every woman is a creature valuable beyond measure—first impacted my heart as I was leading a Bible study with a group of young people at a camp in 1978. By then I had been married for ten years. The reality back then was that I didn't fully appreciate the miracle of what God had given me in my wife, and she felt it. During that camp, as we opened up the Book of Genesis, I said to the young men, "Guys, I want you to turn and look at the girls sitting around you at this camp. Do you realize that they are not just a face and a body? Do you realize that every girl is a profound miracle; each one is valuable beyond your ability to imagine? Every one of them is made in the image of God. Behind that face and inside that body is a being so valuable that God thinks nothing in the world even comes close. A woman is formed in the image of the Creator himself. Every woman is a miracle with thoughts, feelings, hopes, dreams, desires, likes and dislikes; each one is valuable beyond measure."

As I expanded that idea, I was stunned by the realization that I'd never seen my own wife as a miracle—a person formed in the image of God. From that moment it began to dawn on me how profoundly I had been influenced by the media's portrayal of women. My view of women had been influenced by television commercials of girls bouncing down the beach in their bikinis. I had grown up in awe of how outwardly attractive a girl was. So when I finally had one of my own, I had never got beyond the outer package to discover that behind that beautiful face and inside that beautiful body was a person. In ten years of marriage, I had never really connected with that insight; I had never really appreciated what a miracle a woman is.

I went home and, for the first time, I began to look at my wife with different eyes. I began to realize, *Helen is not just a woman—she is a person and she is a miracle!* That revelation began a whole new era in our relationship, because ten years into our marriage I realized how precious she was. I know that doesn't say a lot for my intelligence!

You must guard your heart with this truth: A woman is a miracle, formed in the image of God. To be given the privilege of sharing your life with this miracle is a privilege you must value as extraordinary. Decide you will guard that miracle with everything in you; honor her, value her, treasure her, tremble at the thought of what a priceless jewel has been put in your hands. It will guard your heart.

Principle 4: What God has given me is profoundly fragile

Not only do you have the privilege of living life with a woman of incredible value, you also are living life with somebody who is profoundly fragile. In many ways, women are strong beyond belief. I was present for the birth of three of my four children. If men had babies there wouldn't be many of them! There is a strength and robustness in womankind that takes the breath away. At the same time, the heart of a woman is a fragile thing. Women are hurt, demeaned, wounded and lessened when men don't fully appreciate what a miracle they have in a wife, so we must revisit the Ewe Lamb Principle once more.

Below is a photo of my wife at the age of two. She is riding a little rocking horse in the backyard of the newly constructed family home with one of her dolls in front of her feet. Just two years after this photo was taken, her mother was diagnosed with cancer, and this commenced a chain of tragic events in her home life that has marked her to this day. In that same backyard at the age of four, Helen had her first spiritual encounter with the presence of God. She says her encounter with the presence of God was so real that it lives with her to this day. As a little child, God visited her, and she was aware of his presence. At that moment she loved him and wanted to know him more. This photograph of my wife stands on my study desk as a powerful daily reminder of my responsibilities as a *valiant man*. Something profoundly valuable has been placed in my hands for safe keeping: She is vulnerable and fragile, and I must take care of her.

In a previous chapter we talked about the story—in 2 Samuel, Chapter 11—when David looked over his balcony and saw Bathsheba taking a bath. As he peered down at this woman, his testosterone-fueled sexuality kicked in and the chemistry set in his head began to do its thing. Phenylethylamine shot into his system and before he knew it he had a raging lust for her. He sent for her, vented his sexual passions on her, got her pregnant, and then murdered her husband to cover up the act.

You would think a man capable of such behavior must be devoid of moral fiber. Not so; his moral core had been submerged under a flood of sexual chemistry, but God showed up through Nathan the prophet with a story designed to get past the testosterone fog and bring that moral core to the surface. The story went like this:

And the Lord sent Nathan to David. He came to him and said to him, "There were two men in a certain city, the one rich and the other poor. The rich man had very many flocks and herds, but the poor man had nothing but one little ewe lamb, which he had bought. And he brought it up, and it grew up with him and with his children. It used to eat of his morsel and drink from his cup and lie in his arms, and it was like a daughter to him. Now there came a traveler to the rich man, and he was unwilling to take one of his own flock or herd to prepare for the guest who had come to him, but he took the poor man's lamb and prepared it for the man who had come to him." Then David's anger was greatly kindled against the man, and he said to Nathan, "As the Lord lives, the man who has done this deserves to die, and he shall restore the lamb fourfold, because he did this thing, and because he had no pity." Nathan said to David, "You are the man!"[115]

---

115   2 Samuel 12:1-7 The Message Bible

It was as if God was saying, "David, you've had an attitude to women all your life. Your attitude to women is that they are cattle that exist just to meet your needs. So you use them like cattle, and you've had quite a few of them." As a matter of fact, at that moment David had six wives and a cluster of concubines on the side. You can see that David's son, Solomon, began his slippery slide to having a multitude of women by observing his father.

Through Nathan, God said to David, "You saw a woman and she stirred your sexuality, but I saw inside that woman. I saw the same fragile child that I formed in her mother's womb. I created her to be respected by men, to be honored by men, and to be guarded by a man. Yet you have done none of these things. You have treated her like a meal, and you have put her to the knife for your own pleasure." What follows this story is a stern rebuke. Every one of us should read it and take it to heart.

There is nobility deep in the heart of most men that is moved to fight for the weak and defend the defenseless. That story about that little lamb cut through David's testosterone fog and brought his manly nobility and sense of justice to the surface. That story about the ewe lamb has done the same to me. It has influenced me as much as anything I have ever heard or read about men's attitudes to women. My wife, that little ewe lamb, entrusted her happiness and her future into my hands when she committed herself to be married to me. She had alternatives, and believe me, so did your wife! You weren't the only show in town! I don't care who you are or how handsome you think you are, you were not the only option.

When your wife gave her love to you, her destiny, her happiness and her future were placed in your hands. I don't know what that does for you, but that stirs in me a deep sense of responsibility and the recognition that, by God, I had better not disappoint her. One day God is going to want to talk to me about how well I managed that responsibility, and I want to be able to hand my wife back to God in better shape than when she came to me. I want to be able to say to Him, "Lord, she was a profound blessing! I have guarded her and kept her. You gave me a treasure and I have honored the gift you gave me in my ewe lamb."

I want to encourage you to find a photograph of your wife when she was a child and carry it around with you or place it where you can see it every day. That may be in your wallet, on your office desk, or beside your bed. I've got three of them. I've had them blown up into a large size. The one printed in this book stands on my office desk. Cherish that picture and have it readily available for your own nurture and for the adjustment of your heart. It will help to clear the testosterone fog from time to time and remind you that this precious and delicate treasure was trusted into your hands by the grace of God.

Principle 5: I was born to be an ox and a lion

As men, God has put before us the challenge to *abad* and *shamar*. In chapter 1, I explained that the Hebrew word *abad* means "to work", "to labor" and "to serve." We saw that one of the four qualities a man is called to embrace is that of an ox. Adam was told to work and to take care of the garden God had given him. In other words, he was to work, labor and serve in the garden.

One of the reasons that testosterone is your hormonal driver is that it makes your muscular mass 40% of your body weight (if you're in good shape, that is!), compared to a woman whose muscle mass is 23 percent of her body weight. You were designed to be stronger, bigger and more powerful because, like the ox, you were designed to carry burdens on her behalf. Get a job, pay bills, mow lawns, provide for your family, carry parcels, buy her presents, open doors, and do it all quietly and willingly. It's your job.

On the other hand, you were also called by God to *shamar*, which means "to guard", "to keep" and "to protect". A man is called to be a lion, whose chief role is to *shamar*. I believe your heart will be happiest when you sense that you are fulfilling the calling of the lion and the ox on your wife's behalf. As the man, you must embrace your call to be the head of your wife and to love her as Christ loved the Church. As such, you must accept the challenge to give leadership in sacrifice and in love.

As a lion it is your calling to stand up and guard your household. Establish in your thought life a clear conviction that your strength and size will never be used to bring fear into your own home. No angry, violent nonsense, just because you are big and scary. Set your heart to guard your kids from anyone who would want to rip them off. Set your heart to provide a safe haven in your home. Let it be that because of you, your wife and children will live securely every day of their lives.

Principle 6: I will honor the pinnacle of God's creation

A woman is the crown of God's creation. Women love to tell the joke that when God created man on the sixth day, He looked at him and said, "Mmmm, I think I can do a little better than that." So out of the man's side God took a rib and built a woman. Woman is the last and the greatest act of creation.

She is a picture of the beauty God sees coming out of this world. She is typical of the beauty of a people whom he calls the Bride of Christ. Out of all of the roughness of life God wanted to create a treasure, so he created a woman. She is so spectacular that he calls her the crown of his creation and the glory of man. She may be the weaker vessel in terms of muscular strength, but as I said before, if you've ever been around for the birth of a child you'll want to prostrate yourself and worship the ground she walks on. If men had to carry and give birth to babies, there wouldn't be many of them!

I never cease to be moved by the courage of women, by their ability to stick around when men give up and walk away. When Jesus died on the cross, the only people left were women. The only people who turned up on that Sunday morning to anoint his body for burial were women. It's not uncommon at the end of the life cycle of a church that the last few worshipers left before they turn off the lights for good are women. Women often persevere when we men have had enough and have walked away.

A woman is a spectacular creature. God calls the woman a *helper*.[116] The word he uses for *helper* is a word he uses about himself when he calls himself the helper of Israel.[117] To call the woman a helper isn't to say that she is inferior. Rather, it means that she is superior. If you're going to get help from someone, then they must be able to do something you can't, otherwise they wouldn't be of any help to you. That's why God calls himself Israel's helper. In effect, he says, "I can do for Israel what Israel cannot do for herself." When God created woman, he created her with strengths and capacities that are greater than yours in so many ways. She is a magnificent creature. So honor her. Honor every woman you ever meet. She is the crown of God's creation. For her sake, guard your heart and determine that you will keep your body in holiness and in honor.

Principle 7: Only room for one in the corral of my heart

As I have said a number of times throughout this book, sex is glue. In 1 Corinthians the Apostle Paul says:

Do you not know that he who unites himself with a prostitute

116   Genesis 2:18
117   Psalm 33:20

is one with her in body? For it is said, "The two will become one flesh." But he who unites himself with the Lord is one with him in spirit. Flee from sexual immorality. All other sins a man commits are outside his body, but he who sins sexually sins against his own body.[118]

God created sex out of the ability of one spirit to join with another spirit and to transmit life change through that intimacy. Now, because God got the idea for sex from that capacity—when two people come together—sex has the ability to make changes in us that are permanent. It's one of the reasons why sexual immorality impacts mankind so profoundly.

Let me repeat something I've said before. I've never yet had a man present at the altar for prayer who has said to me, "Could you pray for me because 15 years ago I was playing football and someone punched me in the eye. I've been so upset by that incident that I've never been able to get over it." I've never heard anybody say that to me, but I have had many people ask for prayer saying, "Years ago I was sexually abused and I've never been able to get over it." There is something about sexual misconduct that is different to the misuse of any other part of our body. If you touch a person sexually in an inappropriate way, they can still be dealing with the pain of that incident 50 years later. It's because sex has the ability to change us. Sex is glue and it sticks people together; it sticks us to experiences and emotions as well.

Sex is so powerful that an act of past immorality doesn't just need forgiveness, it needs healing: Things that have been inappropriately stuck together need to be unstuck and things that were once tied together inappropriately need to be untied. Sometimes

---

118   1 Corinthians 6:16-18

things that we once held very close to ourselves have a painful memory that still occupies a place in our heart.

A *valiant man* understands that there is only room for one woman in his heart. For that reason, if you want to be a *valiant man*, you have to empty your heart of old girlfriends, old dreams and old hopes. You have got to put to death the romances of the past and the dream that you could have had someone better. I had a friend who didn't do that. He had within his heart a hope to be loved by a woman other than the one to whom he was married. Today he is no longer in ministry. He would not empty his heart of the hope for a different kind of woman and eventually it undermined his marriage relationship. Don't do that.

A *valiant man* lives in the present, not in the past or in a fantasy world. You must free your mind from old flames and old attractions. A wild donkey needs a corral or an enclosure when the heat is on. If you've had your passions inflamed by another woman, you have got to bring that heart back into the corral and ensure that your heart is in a place that it is kept for one person alone. Throw all others out of your corral. Expel every other hope and dream. Deal with yourself. Be strong. Be violent with any foreign affection that attempts to make a little nest in a corner of your heart.

As men, we are stirred visually. So one of the great dangers we face is that when we meet beautiful, attractive women throughout our week, there is real potential for us to let a woman other than our wife into our heart. This is especially true for those of those who work with women and are surrounded by them. In an atmosphere where people are encouraging one another, supporting one another, sharing their hearts and dreams with one another, it's very easy for a door to open in our heart—in our corral—and to let someone else walk in and begin to occupy a place they have no right to occupy.

When someone who attracts you enters your world, the flags have to go up. Defenses must be immediately activated. If that happens to you, put your shield up very quickly. You must be aware that that attraction is a threat to everything precious in your life. If you start living in a fantasy world with this other person, setting up a dual-focus or a multi-focus in your mind, you will diminish, destroy and damage the love and connectedness you have with the one woman God has given you. Your Master gave you your wife, so you have no right to entertain unclean or unrighteous thoughts about another woman. You have a responsibility to bounce your eyes away from that person. Avoid her rather than build a rapport with her. Put some distance between you. Don't let it go any further. Hold your ground until the attraction dies; and believe me it will.

One of the reasons I've been moved to create the Valiant Man program and write this book is that I am so grateful to be a survivor. I've never lowered my flag of integrity and I'm in love with the girl I married in 1968, but I've felt the heat of the battle. What I'm about to share with you is one of the most important experiences of my life.

Many years ago I found myself attracted to someone who was working in my sphere of influence. She was a decent woman and none of what unfolded had anything to do with provocative or flirtatious behavior. She never acted inappropriately and neither did I, but for some reason I just found myself attracted to her. She will never know the struggle I went through, but for a year I had to take a stand against the inappropriate attraction I felt towards her. My lying emotions got into the act and tried to convince me I could never be happy unless I pursued a relationship with her. I guess it was just the "love map" thing which triggered some unhelpful phenylethylamine bio-chemistry… and I was struggling.

I had a number of things going for me in that dangerous season (and I still do): I really feared God and I truly believed the Bible. I knew that the Bible says the heart of man is deceitful above all things[119]. I would continually say to my heart and to my emotions: *You are a liar. If I chase that woman I will end up ashamed, disappointed, empty and broken. I refuse to give this a place in my life.* The fear of God kept me from telling myself it could somehow be okay to act on the attraction and destroy both her life and her marriage. Added to that, I have a total life commitment to my Ewe Lamb, which made it unthinkable to wound my wife and damage our relationship.

However, the emotional battle was so fierce and relentless I eventually had to seek support from my wife and my then Senior Pastor for fear that I might act foolishly and damage a whole circle of related individuals. It was one of the most embarrassing self-revelations I have ever had to make. However I felt the only responsible thing I could do was to humble myself, tell the truth, and ask for help.

Helen was magnificent. She fronted up like a warrior and declared, "This is an attack on both of us and we are going to fight it together!" My Senior Pastor was magnificent and fathered me strongly through the following months. Nothing anybody did actually helped, but because I'd told the truth I was able to hold my ground and I stood resolutely against that wrong affection for a whole year. I wondered if my emotions would ever come into line, but eventually they did. That inappropriate affection is not only dead, but when I see that woman today I ask myself: *What on earth were you thinking?!* I couldn't get back in touch with those emotions today in any way, shape or form. I am a survivor. No, wait... I'm

---

119   Jeremiah 17:9

more than a survivor—I'm an overcomer! I'm passionately in love with my wife, and she is proud of me. I'm her *valiant man.*

If another woman has found a place in your heart, you have to fight to get her out. You have got to realize that everything you value is under threat in those moments. A *valiant man* fights for the integrity of his own heart. I'm not here today because I'm a perfect man. Far from it! I'm alive and well to tell the story because I have taken a stand and the principles I'm sharing with you come from the Word of God—so they work! Guard your heart with this conviction: There is only room for one woman in this heart of mine.

Principle 8: Roll out the red carpet

The goal of your restoration is to have a new heart—a heart in which you love your wife passionately, as Christ loves the Church. It's a love without a limit, and where no price is too high when it comes to being a *valiant man.* That kind of love demands expression and one of the best ways to communicate to yourself and to your wife the value you place on her is the "red carpet" treatment. Do something extravagant for your wife and do it often. Every time you roll out the red carpet you reinforce just how special she is.

The Bible says:

Husbands, love your wives, just as Christ loved the church and gave himself up for her to make her holy, cleansing her by the washing with water through the word, and to present her to himself as a radiant church, without stain or wrinkle or any other blemish, but holy and blameless. In this same way, husbands ought to love their wives as their own bodies. He who loves his wife loves himself. After all, no one ever hated his own body, but he *nourishes* and *cherishes* it, just as Christ does the church—for we are members of his body. For this reason a man will leave his father and mother and be united to his wife, and the two will become one flesh.[120]

To *nourish* means "to care for", "to feed", "to provide for", and "to raise up". That word *nourish* is often used to describe a parent's care for a child. Now, your wife is not a child, but it brings us back to the Ewe Lamb Principle: *I'm willing to lay down my life for her. I will serve her, protect her and care for her. She is worthy of that kind of commitment.*

To *cherish* means "to soften by heat" and "to keep warm". It refers to the nurturing act of a mother bird covering her young with her feathers. That is a beautiful perspective. A woman wants to be profoundly loved. Your wife wants to be profoundly loved by you… softly, with words, actions, touch and attention. It can be done in a thousand different ways. This beautiful word, "to soften by heat", encourages us to believe that if we're disappointed with the level of intimacy we are currently experiencing with our wives things can improve; over time she can be softened by heat. I'm not talking about the heat of arguments, but the warmth of kindness and affectionate attention. This is a promise to every *valiant man*.

So roll out the red carpet for your ewe lamb. The Song of Solomon is a picture of passion focused in the right place. Take a leaf out of the pages of the Song of Solomon. It's a picture of passionate, extravagant and overt expressions of love for your wife. Roll out the red carpet. Warm her heart and soften it by extravagant expressions of love. The world needs to see the nature of Christ in the way we roll out the red carpet for our brides. It will do more to make Christ credible in our broken world than a wordy argument ever could.

---

120   Ephesians 5:25-31

REFLECTION

My friend, I believe these eight principles have the power to help you guard your heart and, over time, to enhance your affections towards your wife. I have experienced a number of seasons in my life in which my affections have drifted in the wrong direction. I have experienced seasons in my life in which my affections have dropped to a lower level than they needed to be. But every time I have paid attention to these issues, my affections were nurtured and fanned into flame again. So I encourage you to make a decision to guard your eyes, guard your thoughts, and guard your heart. For in so doing, you will become a *valiant man.*

CHAPTER 10

REALISTIC EXPECTATIONS

"What saves a man is to take a step. Then another step."
Antoine De Saint-Exupery

"Success is the ability to go from one failure to another with
no loss of enthusiasm."
Sir Winston Churchill

A *valiant man* is willing to have a go. A *valiant man* is prepared to go to war, to confront danger, to pay the price, and to take on the battles that are necessary to see good triumph over evil. My friend, the fact that you are reading this book through to the last chapter demonstrates that something in you wants to be a *valiant man* and for that I commend you.

Personal purity is part of God's plan for your life. He wants you to mature in the management of your male sexuality, to grow from *good* man to *valiant* man. God puts it so simply in this one verse from the Bible: "But among you there must not be even a hint of sexual immorality, or of any kind of impurity."[121] Remember, the Bible also says, "It is God's will that you should be sanctified: that you should avoid sexual immorality; that each of you should learn to control his own body in a way that is holy and honorable."[122]

Now, that's a lot easier said than done in a society that hammers you with eroticism and with sexualized communication 24 hours a day. Pornography peeps at you from the shelves of almost every news agency across the country, from late night television programs in your family room, and even from billboards on sidewalks in broad daylight. During every waking moment you and I are under pressure to become impure men. It seems that society does not want to give us a chance at personal purity.

However, rest assured that the core strength of the valiant man is his relationship with his God, for he knows that his God is for him and with him all the days of his life. That's why the man seeking purity has got to nurture moments of intimacy with God, moments in which he opens his heart, his life and his motivations to the presence of God's Spirit. Jesus said, "I stand at the door and knock. If anyone hears my voice and opens the door, I will come in

---

121   Ephesians 5:3
122   1 Thessalonians 4:3-4

and eat with him, and he with me."[123] The *valiant man* embraces that promise and opens his heart to Jesus continually.

Out of intimacy with God's Spirit the human spirit has the power to will what is right in a way that it can never do in isolation. Sometimes I just lie on the carpet in the dark and do my best to be open to God. Alone with Him in the dark, I tell Him, "I need you! Draw near to me. Take who I am and make me like you." It's in those moments of intimacy that I experience a subtle change within that gives me the power and desire to will what is right in a way I could never experience if left to myself. It works for *me*. Try it *yourself* and see what happens.

As we come to the final pages of this journey together, I want to leave you with realistic expectations about your personal purity. It's very important that you have realistic expectations. People become damaged when their expectations are not met. It makes them feel that God is not interested in them, that perhaps they are defective individuals. To strive for purity and feel that you have missed the mark because of unrealistic expectations will only hinder your journey from *good* man to *valiant* man.

Realistic expectations support the healing process. Unrealistic expectations set us up for failure, and we didn't start the journey from *good* man to *valiant man* to fail. It's important that when you put this book down at the last page you have a realistic hope for the future. I want to leave you with four realistic expectations and a challenge from the words of Winston Churchill: "Never give in, never give in—never, never, never, never." The only failure is in walking away from the challenge.

Realistic Expectation 1: Your sex drive will not go away

Men are endowed with a strong and relentless sex drive. You

---

123   Revelation 3:20

have got to face the fact that your sex drive will not go away simply because you have picked up this book, read every page, and applied every principle. That's right! Your sex drive will not go away, and you won't be able to pray it away either. It's important for you to recognize that you have been designed by your Creator with a strong and relentless sex drive. When you feel it impinging on your life and pressuring you, it's not because you are a bad or impure man, it is simply because you are a man. You may have learned a great deal in this book. It may have improved your marriage, and it may have alerted you to the issues involved, but this book will not stop your sex drive from thundering away inside you and making its demands on you.

There are many reasons for the continuing pressure of your sex drive. Physiologically nothing has changed: You have an inbuilt testosterone engine, your body is a sperm factory, and your brain has been hardwired for sexual arousal. So don't be surprised if your body continues to want to rule your life. Reading this book will not change that. However, what this book *will* do is it will provide you with some understanding about how to master your sex drive. You have been endowed with a high potential for sexual pleasure, but with that privilege comes a high responsibility to discipline your body.

So, your first realistic expectation should be: *My sex drive is not going to go away.* However, the good news is that you can learn to manage your sex drive in such a way that it becomes the blessing that it was intended to be. A *valiant man* determines that this cluster of challenges and potentialities are going to function in obedience to God, even in the midst of pressure, difficulty, pain and struggle. A *valiant man* realizes that suffering is at least part of God's plan to bring into being great men and great women. If you don't believe me that suffering is part of God's plan, then read the Book of James where it says, "Consider it pure joy, my brothers, whenever you face trials of many kinds."[124] The Bible also says, "When he has tested me, I will come forth as gold."[125] Jesus learned obedience through the things he suffered, and so will you if you have the courage to lean into the challenge and be the man you are.

Your sex drive is a part of the challenge of life. There'll be days when your sex drive will cause you to feel frustration, pain and difficulty, but if you master it there will be moments when you experience the full thrill of sexual intimacy knowing that there is no shame, knowing that there is no guilt, and knowing that you are experiencing what God intended. If you will live wisely and accept the struggle that comes with having a male sex drive you can also experience its benefits, and out of that struggle the character that God is seeking to produce in you will be revealed in its entire splendor. God is more concerned about your character than your comfort. That's why He has given you some things to wrestle with. So do it manfully and you'll be rewarded in many ways.

Realistic Expectation 2: Change takes time and obedience

The second realistic expectation is that change takes time and it takes obedience. God moves slowly. Discipleship is rarely rapid and it usually involves a measure of suffering. The reality is that habits take time to change. You may not yet have mastered everything I have outlined in this book, but that does not mean that you are a bad man; it simply means you're a man on a journey. It takes you ten years to be ten years old. A five-year-old cannot suddenly grow

---

124   James 1:2
125   Job 23:10

into a ten-year-old by trying harder. You have to live for ten years before you can become ten years of age.

In the same way, you are not yet fully mature because that is going to take time. When you follow human experience throughout the Bible you see how normal it is for men who pursue God to face challenges. The track record of believers throughout history demonstrates that God expects them to face their challenges like men, and to have a go. Hebrews chapter 11 provides a list of believers who discovered that pursuing the best can be very painful and very expensive, but the reward is out of this world. Listen to the counsel of Hebrews Chapter 12 as it challenges us to face our struggles:

> Let us fix our eyes on Jesus, the author and perfecter of our faith, who for the joy set before him endured the cross, scorning its shame, and sat down at the right hand of the throne of God. Consider him who endured such opposition from sinful men, so that you will not grow weary and lose heart. In your struggle against sin, you have not yet resisted to the point of shedding your blood. [126]

You may be saying today: *This struggle against masturbation is killing me!* Well, it hasn't killed you yet. And until it does, you haven't over exerted yourself. *How hard should I try?* you ask. Well, Jesus went to the point of death to face his struggles. You haven't had to go that far, so stop moaning about it. Take up the challenge. Be prepared to have a go, and face the pain, suffering and opposition that go with it. Take it like a man. Face it like a man. Sexual discipleship is no different to any other challenge. God expects you to make decisions and he expects you to exercise commitment.

---

126   Hebrews 12:2-4

God has promised that your decisions to act in obedience to his Word will meet with a divine response. When you're struggling, and when your path is difficult, painful and inconvenient, you are still called to press on and to persist. Being willing to struggle is proof that God is still at work inside you.

You are not Robinson Crusoe. You are not alone. You are not the only man struggling with issue of personal purity. I am transparent about my own struggles because I figure that if I can tell you the truth maybe you can too. If we were all to do that, we would discover that the Church is actually a meeting of Sinners Anonymous. The Church is not a bunch of unchallenged and non-struggling individuals who have taken a pill called *faith* or a dose of the Jesus solution so that all their problems are solved.

Our willingness to fight is more exciting to God than our perfection. It's not so much a matter of how far you've progressed, but in which direction you're travelling.

There will continue to be moments when you'll fail. That doesn't mean you can give yourself permission to fail and then brush off failure as if it doesn't matter. However, having said that, I don't expect to perfectly live out the principles in my own book and never again face a challenge. Every man with realistic expectations has to face the fact that he is going to fail again sooner or later. You will not live out your life perfectly.

My question to you, therefore, is this: What are you going to do when you do fail again? You see, you won't grow without mistakes. A child does not learn to walk without falling down, getting up, and falling down again. Whatever you are learning to do, if you keep doing it you'll get better at it. Finishing the race is not about perfection. If you begin a ten kilometer bike ride and after just three kilometers you fall off, you don't have to go back to the start and begin again. No, you can get up off the ground, get back on your bike at the three kilometer mark, and keep pedaling. If you fall off at the seven kilometer mark, just get back on your bike and pick up the pace again. You don't need to stop or go back to the start if you fail. You don't have to ride a perfect race to finish, you just have to persevere and get back up every time you fall. A realistic expectation is that you will fall off at some time and at some place. You will continue to make mistakes along your journey. There will be moments when you think: *Oh no, I didn't handle that well!* Just get up again, hop on your bike, and keep going.

Realistic Expectation 3: Healing takes time and obedience

Healing also takes time. It's going to take time to restore the damage. Every one of us needs to recognize that the distortions in our sexuality may have caused significant damage in a variety of ways. Reading this book doesn't mean all the damage you may have caused in your sphere of influence is undone. Your marriage may have been wounded by your behavior. Your wife may have been sadly impacted in one way or another. Your church may have been impacted. Your children may have been affected. Your home life may have been damaged. All of that is not going to be repaired just because you've read this book or taken part in the ten week Valiant Man program.

A word of caution at this point could really help you. At the end of each Valiant Man program in our church, we host an evening event to which the men can bring their wives to hear an overview of what the course has covered. This is important because it gives the wives an understanding about how they can work together with their husband on the healing journey. It's not uncommon during this evening event to see how pained some of the women are;

they've been wounded by the impact of poorly handled sexuality. For the husband, the penny has finally dropped. He's bright-eyed and bushy-tailed about the future, down on one knee and ready to serve as a *valiant man*. I've seen the pain and the hurt in the eyes of more than one woman—defensive and suspicious about how this will really work out for her. Healing for her is going to take more than a promise and a red rose. You have to give her time.

Often a woman doesn't understand her man's struggle with his sexuality. She may never have appreciated that a man's sexuality is more of a challenge for him than her sexuality is for her. When a wife discovers that her husband has had a struggle with personal purity it's possible for her to feel as betrayed as if her husband has had an affair. Sometimes significant rebuilding of emotional trust and intimacy needs to take place. It's going to take time and you need to be prepared to do the work.

You may have allowed things into your home, movies and entertainment that have defiled you and lowered the whole spiritual tone of your home. If so, that has to be restored, and you can't just restore it by telling everybody that things are going to be different from now on. You have to prove it to others and to yourself. You have to demonstrate it with a track record over time.

It's possible that your lower standards in the recent past have damaged your prayer life and the way you do home devotions. Often, when a man begins to feel his integrity slipping away, he feels he can't pray; he feels like a hypocrite if he reads his Bible in front of his family; he feels he can't be a spiritual leader. If that has been the case with you, then the lowering of your standards has damaged your family. That will take time to restore, and it needs to be restored carefully, not in a sudden burst of arrogance or in an urgent and forced display of spirituality. Restoration needs to be nurtured and encouraged with gentleness and integrity.

You need to be consistent in the rebuilding of your life while your changed attitude and your healthy behavior begin to elevate the home again. It may be that worship music and conversation about spiritual matters have disappeared from your home. If that's the case, then your home may be spiritually depleted. You may have invested very little energy in building a warm spiritual environment in your own home. Well, that's going to take time to restore. It's my prayer that your personal restoration will flow over into your home until it becomes a household restoration.

If you will persist in cleansing your life, two things will take place. First, you'll begin to sense lightness and a joy returning to your soul. You'll once again sense the dignity of being a good and decent man. Second, you will begin to love your wife more than you've ever loved her before. And the result will be that you'll both discover a fresh delight in your marriage.

Your life can be straightened, just like my teeth need to be straightened. Let me tell you about my teeth. I have crooked bottom teeth. Now, if I wanted my teeth to be straightened, I could pray, *Oh, Jesus, straighten my teeth!* I have no doubt that God can do medical miracles in a person's mouth, but I may find that for the rest of my life my crooked teeth stay exactly as they are. There is no guarantee that God will miraculously straighten my teeth.

However, a dentist could fix my teeth. He could make some braces for me, attach them to my teeth and start tightening the screws. There would be a measure of pain and a lot of visits, but if I was willing a year or eighteen months from now all my bottom teeth would be straight. What may not happen through an instantaneous miracle will most definitely take place through persistence and an investment of time, effort and money.

What a dentist can do with my teeth, God can do with your sexuality. It may not happen through a miracle; there will probably not be a 'laying on of hands' and a brand new experience of sex for you, but if you will persist, you can be straightened too, and that healing process will eventually benefit your whole family.

Realistic Expectation 4: You may not make it if you try to go it alone

You may be struggling with some significant issues, but hopefully by now you've begun to make progress. However, let me warn you that if you try to go it alone, you may not reach full restoration. You may find that with time you forget what you've learned in this book and drift back into old ways. My friend, I'm sure you don't want to find yourself sliding back to where you were before you started this book. The truth is that whilst this book won't fix all your problems it is intended to launch you on a voyage to a new future. However, a good beginning is not the same as a good ending. You need to be realistic about how healthy you are and how capable you are of continuing the journey alone.

When you get an infection in your body, sometimes your own immune system is able to rise up and overcome that infection. At other times, when an infection gets into your body, you realize that your body can't fight it alone, so you go to the doctor for help. The doctor may stick a needle in your arm to give you a shot of antibiotics. He may do that on a regular basis until the infection disappears. It's a dangerous thing to start a course of antibiotics and not continue with it long enough to actually kill the bug and get healthy again. When you don't complete a course of antibiotics, you're messing with the healing process. You may suppress the infection for a while, but if you walk away from the doctor's course of medication—if you don't follow through to the end—that infection can rebound, and when it does it can hit you worse than before; and that can be fatal.

Morality works in the same way. God has a number of ways to fortify your natural immune system. Counseling can do it; doing the journey with someone who understands your challenges and has the skills to support you can make all the difference. A support group can do it too. It makes a difference when you connect with a group of guys who will sit with you, talk with you, pray alongside you, challenge you, inspire you, visit you, make phone calls to you, and hang with you when you're going through the toughest times. They can fortify your immune system. A church-based home group (or cell group) can help, and a healthy church life can certainly fortify you on the journey as well.

Don't fool yourself. If you know your own immune system is not yet mature enough to manage the ongoing challenge, then you must make a decision today. Be totally honest with yourself. Ask yourself: *Am I well enough now to continue alone? Do I have the control and the level of health to be able to continue practicing the principles in this book without ongoing fortification from others?*

One of the most important questions for you to deal with right now is this: Can you put this book down today saying: *This has been good for me. It has supplemented my natural immune system. God has boosted me. I'm on the right track. I know I'm going to make it?* Or are you amongst a group of other men who should honestly say to themselves: *This has been a good beginning, but it's not yet a good ending. I do need to be supported. I do need to have an ongoing experience of accountability.* If that's you, then I urge you to find support, whether it's counseling, an ongoing men's support group, or by joining a Valiant Man program in your area -find a Valiant Man program in your area by visiting the website: www.careforcelifekeys.org

In conclusion, let me say this to you. Life is short and eternity is long. Growing from *good* man to *valiant* man is not just about having a better life; it's about preparing for eternity. The challenges of this life—every one of them—represent opportunities to prepare for eternity. When *good* men become *valiant* men, they not only tackle issues for life, they tackle them for eternity. When *good* men become *valiant* men, everyone around them is touched for eternity. For Jesus' sake, for the sake of the women and children in your sphere of influence, for your own sake, for the sake of everyone whose life will be touched by you from here to eternity… do the journey—become a *valiant man.*

ACKNOWLEDGEMENTS

There are so many people to whom I owe a debt of gratitude for the existence of this book. Here are but a few:

Firstly to my wife Helen: for loving me, for believing in me, and for a lifetime of encouragement and courageous support. This book is her story as well. It could never have been written had she not been so courageous at key moments in the battle.

To Pastor Hal Oxley whose character and honesty have inspired me ever since we met. Hal Oxley was the first Christian leader I ever heard speak transparently about his own struggles with his sexuality. His moments of personal honesty during a leadership retreat not only inspired me personally but helped put the stamp of authenticity and transparency on my ministry which I have tried to emulate ever since.

To Steve Beattie, a plumber extraordinaire, who believes in Men's Ministry and supported both my study and the development of the Valiant Man project in so many ways. Steve is one of my heroes.

To Mrs. Susan Grechko, wife of Mike, whose assistance and

wisdom meant so much when time was short and the need urgent during the frenetic year of study and work that produced the original Valiant Man program.

To Peter Brewer for his creative input and brilliant cover design.

To all the men who facilitate Valiant Man small groups and thus become partners in ministry with me every time the Valiant Man program is shared anywhere in the world. You turn the message of this book into a life giving stream. Good on you!

Recommended Books

Here is a list of books I would highly recommend you read and from which I have quoted in this book.

The Bible. Scripture I have quoted was taken from a variety of translations. However, I have mostly quoted from the New International Version (NIV) Copyright © 1973, 1978, 1984 by International Bible Society. Used by permission. All rights reserved.

Stephen Arterburn and Fred Stoeker, *Every Man's Battle* (Nashville: Thomas Nelson Publishers, 2004).

Patrick Carnes, *Out of the Shadows* (Center City, MN: Hazelden, 2001).

Dr. Archibald Hart, *The Sexual Man* (Word Publishing, 1994).

Dr. Archibald Hart, Catherine Hart Weber, and Debra L. Taylor, *Secrets of Eve* (Nashville: Thomas Nelson Publishers, 1994).

Donald Joy, *Bonding: Relationships in the Image of God* (Word Publishing, 1991).

T. & B. LaHaye, *The Act of Marriage* (Grand Rapids: Zondervan Publishing, 1998).

N. Malamuth and E. Donnerstein, *Pornography and Sexual Aggression* (Academic Press, 1986).

Anne Moir and David Jessel, *Brain Sex: The Real Difference Between Men and Women* (New York: Delta, 1992).

T. Weir, *Holy Sex* (New Kensington: Whitaker House, 1999).

D. Weiss, *Sex, Men and God* (Siloam Press, 2002).

Author's note: Every effort has been made to identify copyright holders of extracts in this book. The publishers would be pleased to hear from any copyright holders who have not been acknowledged.

About Careforce Lifekeys

Walk down any street near your church and knock on any 10 doors and you will find marriage dysfunction, separation, divorce, family breakdown, the destructive forces of shame and guilt, performance orientation, addictive cycles, co-dependency, insecurity, self rejection, grief, depression, chemical dependency, sexual abuse, sexual addiction, eating disorders and more.

When Jesus Christ adopted Isaiah 61 as his job description (Luke 4:18, 19), he underlined one of the most basic realities about life—Christ came to heal and restore.

Helping our local communities find Christ through their brokenness remains one of the greatest untapped evangelistic tools available to the Church today.

Careforce Lifekeys programs address the issues of ordinary people, struggling with everyday life, and are a powerful outreach tool. Yet Lifekeys is not just an evangelistic tool, it is also a profoundly important tool for church health and leadership development.

Careforce Lifekeys is both church health and evangelism in the 21st Century.

OTHER CAREFORCE LIFEKEYS PROGRAMS

* Careforce Lifekeys Facilitator Training Program
* Search for Life * Search for Intimacy * Door of Hope
* Man to Man * Woman to Woman * Valiant Man
* Chemically Speaking * New Beginnings * Healthy Lifestyle * Kids with Courage * Parenting with Courag * Making Marriage Better * Youth Search for Life

CONTACT US

Careforce Lifekeys, Australia (Head Office)
PO Box 411, Mt Evelyn
Victoria, Australia, 3140

Ph: +61 3 9736 2273
Web: www.careforcelifekeys.org